The Unapc D0721286

Danita Johnson Hughes's powerful combination of tough love and straight talk make her new book, The Unapologetic Woman, *a must-read for both men and women.*

—Nick Morgan
author of **Power Cues: The Subtle Science of Leading Groups, Persuading Others,** and **Maximizing Your Personal Impact**

The Unapologetic Woman *is a must-read for any women who suffers from what author Danita Johnson Hughes describes as The Sorry Syndrome. Whether you're a leader or plan to be one, you will benefit from the solid insights, ideas, candid stories and suggestions offered in this important book.*

—Susan RoAne
Professional speaker and bestselling author,
How to Work a Room®

The Unapologetic Woman *acknowledges an all too common roadblock that women unconsciously use in and outside of the workplace—we apologize too much and too often in the wrong scenario and for things that don't need an apology. Those 'apologies' can diminish the leadership that women seek. Bravo for her exposure and huge kudos in delivering a roadmap that will open more doors for women in any workplace. She does it with excellent examples from her own leadership and from stories of other women who 'broke through' … little is left out. Read it. Devour it. Implement her recommendations.*

—Judith Briles
author of **Stabotage!** and **Zapping Conflict in the Health Care Workplace**

Danita Johnson Hughes gives a strong voice to issues and concerns women face in the work-place and the rest-of-life-place. She is right on target as she identifies behaviors that are everyday occurrences in organizations. In The Unapologetic Woman, *readers learn the tools to change their mindset, change their presence, and change the results they get. Danita removes the blinders and the rose-colored glasses and becomes absolutely real as she shares the heartbreaks and the victories of women in leadership. She will help you turn apologies into triumphs! This book will be on the "must read" list for every female (and male) executive I coach.*

—Dr. Shirley Garrett, CSP
Communication Strategist, Speaker, and Writer
Stop the Craziness: Simple Life Solutions

The Unapologetic Woman *is enticing to say the least! A great read with chapters of inspiring tales of our challenges and "opportunities" to shine as woman leaders. You will find yourself smiling and acknowledging the truthfulness and introspective reflection of how powerful and confident women can and should be. The book is an inspiration for all women seeking to be leaders or already in leader-ship roles and who can relate to the powerful words of wisdom!! With greatest respect and admiration for Danita Johnson Hughes.*

—Janice L. Ryba
CEO & Administrator, St. Mary Medical Center

un the ^apologetic woman

Leading with Power and Confidence

Dr. Danita Johnson Hughes

The Unapologetic Woman
© Copyright 2017, Dr. Danita Johnson Hughes
All rights reserved.

Books may be purchased in quantity
and/or for special sales by contacting the publisher
or author through the website: www.DrDanitaHughes.com
at email address: Danita@DrDanitaHughes

Publisher: Vitality Ventures Press
Cover and Layout Design: Rebecca Finkel, F + P Graphic Design
Editing: Judith Briles and Peggie Ireland
Publishing Consultant: Judith Briles, the Book Shepherd

Library of Congress Control Number: Data on file
ISBN: (print book) 978-0-9972124-0-2
(e-book) 978-0-9972124-1-9
(audio book) 978-0-9972124-2-6

10   9   8   7   6   5   4   3   2   1

Business | Leadership | Healthcare

First Edition
Printed in USA

To my mother

who encouraged me to

"read a book"

whenever I complained

that I was bored.

Foreword

I am delighted to have encountered Danita Johnson Hughes many years ago in her venture and adventure to become a global leader who now holds the title CEO of an integrated health center, Edgewater Systems. She was then and continues to be a leader who women and men look to for guidance, counsel, example, and inspiration. She is able to help a diverse group from both a seasoned academic perspective but also from the school of hard knocks. Danita's advice has a depth and breadth of street smarts that carries into corporate boardrooms.

She herself has an amazing story of transformation, hope, and triumph growing up around domestic violence and gang wars, eventually dropping out of high school to care for her daughter.

But she decided to take control of her life and not let circumstances dictate what was in store for her. She made a plan for herself, sought good mentors, got back in school and ended up achieving a Ph.D. in Human Services.

She is not an "expert" who talks the talk. She has walked the talk in her stilettos all the way to the top. Her generosity of spirit motivated her to share in this book all that she learned that helped her so that you too can have your own plan, transformation, and triumph.

—Debra Benton
executive coach and author of
The Leadership Mind Switch
(McGraw-Hill)

chapter 1

The Sorry Syndrome

Your voice, and you, have the right
to take up space in a conversation;
claim your positioning within
a group and have an opinion.

It was twenty below zero that Monday morning. I had scheduled a very important meeting with my leadership team for 8:00 a.m. A fierce winter storm had come through during the night. The power had gone out at 1:00 a.m. in my home and it was still out as I was preparing to go to work. Compounding my efforts was the fact that at 6:00 a.m., it was still quite dark. So here I was taking a cold shower, trying to get dressed and put on makeup by candlelight.

As would be expected, as I prepared to leave for work, getting my car out of the garage through a snow-filled driveway proved to be quite a challenge. But, I eventually drove away from home and arrived at work at 8:15 a.m.

I quickly exited my car and entered the building. As I rounded the corner to the boardroom, I abruptly stopped as an equally harried male colleague almost crashed into me. I speak quickly, "I am so sorry." He in turn responds, "No problem. It seems we're both in a hurry."

In hindsight, we both experienced the encounter differently. He thought I was apologizing for being wrong—for almost running into him. On the contrary, my immediate thought was "Wow! We almost collided. It was no one's fault, but I am sorry it happened."

As I hurriedly entered the boardroom, I immediately grabbed a seat and launched into a long apology. It went something like this: "I am so sorry that I'm late. The power went out at home because of the storm. I took a cold shower and got dressed nearly in the dark. I struggled to get out of my driveway and traffic was terrible."

In retrospect, I realized that in my attempt to be considerate of others' feelings and their time, I was over apologizing and inadvertently admitting to doing something wrong. However, in my case the circumstances were unavoidable.

> **The Sorry Syndrome** A form of communication that becomes an unconscious habit and used as a filler, an excuse or for no reason at all. Used by both genders with a higher percentage displayed by females.

Have you ever apologized for being too busy or for being late, even if it was only a minute or two past the time you were to meet with someone? Have you ever apologized for merely asking for help? How about just putting something down in the wrong place?

Do women over-apologize ... or verbalize an excuse when it's unnecessary? Are we women the "sorriest" creatures on earth? Is there a Sorry Syndrome … and if there is, are you a practitioner of it?

Before you start thinking I'm dead wrong, betraying my gender or accusing me of being sexist, there's research that backs my questions up. The University of Waterloo in Ontario conducted two studies and published the results in the journal *Psychological Science*. Both studies back up the premise that women say "sorry" more often than men. It doesn't mean that men aren't willing to apologize. What it does show is that men have a much higher threshold for what they deem "necessary" to apologize for.

It also shows that many women seem to have a compulsive urge to apologize for almost everything, even when it is clearly not necessary. Why is this?

The word "sorry" often becomes so ingrained in the female psyche that it becomes a handy filler word. Not surprisingly, the words "I'm Sorry" are often the first words to flow from our mouths.

> I'm sorry, may I ask a question?
> I'm sorry, I don't mean to interrupt.
> I'm sorry, an issue has come up.
> I'm sorry, I'm late because ...
> I'm sorry; this is a dumb question, but ...

In fact, women sometimes apologize for apologizing. We become sorry for almost everything … and sometimes it actually appears that, as women, we are sorry for our very existence. How did that happen? Why do so many women unwittingly need to apologize for who they are?

Power and perceived stereotypes come into play. Too many times women who are in position of leadership or strive to be are labeled with a slew of adjectives: she's bitchy, a shrew, too aggressive, really pushy, manipulative, etc. You've heard these descriptors used about other women, possibly yourself. The "sorry card" can soften an image for some. In my experience as a leader in health care, the apology is too often used as an unconscious crutch and serves to diminish female power.

> An apology should always be appropriate and deserving.

As women, we tend to want to nurture people and situations, and we want to keep peace and bring about harmony. That works against us. And you. Unwarranted apologies can disempower you and cause you to appear to lack self-confidence. As a result, others may think they can take advantage of you. And believe me, they will.

Most women were conditioned at an early age to soften communication. Was it done so you didn't appear pushy or overly aggressive? In establishing your early value system, your parents might have admonished you for speaking when adults were speaking. It was considered rude and whatever you had to say was considered to be relatively unimportant. No wonder you feel the need to stay out of the way and not be noticed.

As a child, I would often hang out to hear the conversation between my mom and her friends when she was entertaining or when she was talking to one of them on the telephone. After all, I could hear a lot of good, juicy gossip if I hung around and wasn't noticed. If I was detected, my mother would always shoo me away by saying, "This is an adult conversation. Go mind children's business." Of course, I would apologize to her or to her friends and slip away. I was sorry I intruded.

Appropriate Versus Not Necessary

Normally, an apology is offered when you've done something wrong. Apologizing when it is appropriate can go a long way in mending relationships or minimizing conflict. This makes it a good thing. It can soften the blow when you've created a minor transgression or made a mistake. But when things occur for which you are clearly not to blame or you have no control over, saying "I'm sorry" is not an appropriate reaction. It begins to show signs of an embedded insecurity and negates the power of whatever words that follow. For instance, in a social setting you may be quick to apologize for someone else's offense simply to keep the peace. Or, at the grocery store when someone turns their shopping cart in front of you, you may be compelled to offer an apology.

An apology should always be appropriate and deserving. Although you may consider it to be a gesture of politeness or respect, it can also be considered disingenuous, especially when offered too freely and without much thought. It can appear that way whether you intend it to or not. Offered too frequently or too easily, it tends to be devalued and loses its effectiveness.

The unfortunate side of this is that these feelings often follow you into the workplace, causing you to second guess your every word or action. In the workplace, an unwarranted apology can also be seen by others as submissive—someone who is a pushover or easily defeated. By accepting responsibility for the misdeeds of others you undermine your credibility.

In the workplace, your nurturing ways may cause you to want to settle situations to keep everyone happy. When things are not harmonious in the workplace, you may even blame yourself. To resolve conflict or to get along with others, you may resort to accepting responsibility for another's faults. I'm sorry. I'm wrong. You're right. It's my fault. You are admitting to a fallibility, the result of which becomes the forfeiture of your power.

Unless you are able to successfully tackle and manage The Sorry Syndrome, it could impact your relationships, your health and your position in the workplace. Constantly blaming yourself or taking responsibility for inappropriate or offensive behavior by others can be a ticket to a therapy session with a mental health counselor. It can lead to stress or depression. In addition, it can drive persons crazy who have your best interest in mind. After all, they want to see you stand up for yourself with confidence and courage.

Whether it is a matter of conditioning or some other deeply seated emotional predisposition, always feeling the need to apologize or soften a situation when you are not at fault devalues your position. While as a child, you may have had to conform to the cultural stereotypes assigned to you; this type of behavior is not okay or acceptable as adults in the workplace. It can be detrimental to your self-esteem, your health and your ability to fare well on the job.

the checklist

STOP ... Stop apologizing when you aren't wrong. Acknowledge any propensity you have to not offend, make excuses or just using "I'm sorry" as a filler phrase and remove the "I'm sorry" habit. When you do, you will build the skills that you need to become the confident, self-assured woman and leader that you desire to be. Your voice, and you, have the right to take up space in a conversation; claim your positioning within a group and have an opinion.

chapter 2

Challenges Are in Your Midst

Self-esteem is more significant
to overall mental and emotional well-being
than esteem from others.

Why Am I Sorry?

A number of reasons why women tend to over apologize has been suggested through the years. They include such things as:

- Lack of confidence
- To fit in/to be accepted
- Feelings of intimidation by someone or a situation

There are many other reasons that women may feel compelled to apologize too often or unnecessarily. But we will begin by exploring a few of these ideas a bit more thoroughly.

Lack of Confidence

At a recent speaking engagement, I was introduced by another member of my profession as, "My esteemed colleague ..." *Well*, I thought, *that's nice*. But the more I thought about the phrase, the less important I realized it to be.

Certainly most of you would like to be held in high esteem within your profession, among your friends and within your communities. However, all the favorable opinions in the world won't do you much good if your own view is negative. In other words, self-esteem is more significant to overall mental and emotional well-being than esteem from others.

A lack of self-confidence is often associated with low self-esteem, and can often be crippling to one's personal, emotional and professional success. From the University of Illinois at Urbana-Champaign comes the following:

> *Self-confidence is an attitude* which allows individuals to have positive yet realistic views of themselves and their situations. Self-confident people trust their own abilities, have a general sense of control in their lives and believe that, within reason, they will be able to do what they wish, plan and expect.

> *People who are not self-confident* depend excessively on the approval of others in order to feel good about themselves. They tend to avoid taking risks because they fear failure. They generally do not expect to be successful.

When it comes to women, prominent journalists Katty Kay and Claire Shipman have interviewed a number of important and outstanding women over the years. In their research, they have concluded that women are less self-assured than men and that to succeed, confidence matters as much as competence.

Confidence, like competence, is a learned behavior. It requires practice to get good at it. It is not something you are born with. As you were growing up, most of you were taught that children are "to be seen and not heard." As you enter adolescence, girls, much more often than boys, are encouraged to be passive, and not to draw attention to themselves. Being assertive or aggressive, you are taught, is an undesirable trait. After all, it can be deemed as offensive, and you certainly don't want to threaten or alienate all those men out there who have the ability to impact the trajectory of your life.

> Confidence is about having an appreciation of your own abilities and qualities.

So, What Exactly Is Confidence?

Simply put, confidence is knowing who you are, what you're good at, and the value you bring to any given interaction or experience. Confidence is about having an appreciation of your own abilities and qualities. It is a state of mind that reflects how you feel about yourself and how you convey that self-perception to others.

When you know who you are, you understand and appreciate your self-worth. You have a clear, realistic understanding of what motivates you and what makes you happy.

You understand your personality, strengths, weaknesses, values, and goals. You are comfortable in your own skin.

This does not necessarily mean that you are totally satisfied with where you are in life and what you've accomplished. Instead, this knowledge may provide you with a sense of self-awareness that drives you to continue to try and be the best you can in your life's pursuits. As a human being you are a unique individual with many nuances. As you grow in self-awareness, you change over time. Most people continue to gain self-awareness and insight throughout their entire lives. And so, you are continually evolving and transforming yourself as you grow.

> Whatever your particular circumstance, you are you in how you act and what you do.

Confidence is not just a matter of knowing who you are, but owning it and being proud of it. When you own it, you understand who you are and you make no apologies for that. In fact, it creates in you a sense of pride and, so, you speak proudly about it. You don't try to explain who you are and why you are that way. It means that everything inherent in you, your likes, dislikes, personality, behaviors, perceptions and feelings, are uniquely yours. They make you who you are, and you are completely at peace with that. You are simply you and there is no need to apologize for it.

For instance, to others you may be nervous, talkative or soft-spoken. You may be viewed as unorthodox, different, maybe even competent or confident. Whatever your particular circumstance, you are you in how you act and what you do, and that is the essence of who you are. The best thing that you can do is embrace it and then move forward, giving your all to realizing your full potential. After that, let the chips fall where they may.

But, let's face it, when it comes to self-confidence, some women have it and some don't. The media is full of examples of women who exude self-confidence. Television, print media, and radio, all inundate you with stories of competent, confident, powerful women who are living lives of happiness and contentment. These are women from all walks of life, politics, sports, and entertainment who always appear so calm and self-assured, even under pressure. You might even ask yourself, "How does she do that? What's her secret?" These women have learned to successfully handle situations and challenges that would likely send most of you into a tizzy.

For women in a predicament of not believing that they amount to much, building self-confidence is not an easy task. As stated previously, you are socialized to believe that you are not worthy, that you are not as good or as smart as the males in your life and that as a female you have "your place." Early on girls are taught to be perfect, to not ruffle any feathers, to be "a good girl." As you grow older, you learn that sometimes you have to ruffle feathers, you have to stick up for yourself, and you have to say what's on your mind. But years of conditioning doesn't make this realization easy to put into practice. By falling victim to the thoughts of others, you surrender control of your life to them and render yourself powerless in your ability to affect change in your life.

But you are not defined by your circumstances or what others think of you. Your position in life, whether you are wealthy or poor, college graduate or high school dropout, does not define who you are. How you respond to the challenges that are presented by your circumstances is the real test. How you take these challenges and turn them into personal accomplishments and successes speaks to who you are. It speaks to your character. These defining moments reveal the real you.

Fear of Success

An area frequently missed in discussions on leadership has to do with the "fear of success." You are all familiar with the concept of fear of failure. In fact, it is frequently discussed as a contributing factor to low self-esteem. But how many of you have given consideration to fear of success as a factor when it comes to women's advancement?

The theory of fear of success was first introduced by psychologist Matina Horner in a research study she undertook to evaluate women's motivation for success. Horner looked at why some women had high anxiety levels, and she hypothesized that the possibility of success invoked a great deal of apprehension in these women. In her interpretation of the results of her study, she summarized that the fear of success in women was completely rational: "Fear of success is not neurotic. It's a realistic appraisal of what society has taught us and how society has responded to women."

The fear of success, although more common in women, is a problem with men as well. Actor Dustin Hoffman was once asked in a television interview if he had any regrets. He responded that he regretted having turned down a number of roles for movies that subsequently did quite well at the box office. When asked why he opted not to accept a role in the production of what he knew to be a brilliant script, with a brilliant director, and that he felt strongly would likely be a great movie, he simply replied, "I was afraid of success." So you see, the fear of success is very real!

Hearing someone say "I'm afraid of success" seems counterintuitive. In fact, you have probably never heard it said because it is so rare. However, it is a real fear and is actually quite common. The fear of success can cause you to miss out on opportunities that might come your way. It causes you to be afraid to take risks and set achievable goals. The fear of success can cause you to get stuck in a place of complacency—a place that feels safe and that does not threaten your comfort level.

So, how do you overcome the behaviors associated with fearing success? The truth is you are your biggest obstacle. The fear of success is akin to self-sabotage. It is often unconscious, but the result is you fail to reach your full potential. The problem is that it causes you to settle for mediocrity, to not challenge yourself, and to make up excuses as to why you aren't able to move forward on an important project or initiative. The fact is, you are standing in your own way.

Some signs that you might be afraid of success include:

- You feel that you don't deserve to be successful. Others close to you—family, friends—may not have achieved a similar level of success thus invoking feelings of guilt in you.

- You play small because you are afraid that others may be jealous of your accomplishments or you don't want to be noticed.

- You don't want to get your hopes up for fear you might fail. So therefore you don't aggressively pursue your dreams and passions.

- If you are successful and can't sustain it, others will think badly of you and talk negatively about you.

- You frequently fail to complete projects, or things go wrong when you are near completion.

- You are often embarrassed to talk about your accomplishments or to have others talk about them in your presence.

- You're afraid that success will change you and that you will no longer be accepted in your same circles.

- You feel that success is not possible for you.

- You seek to avoid conflict with others in your life.

The following are ten tips for building self-confidence and avoiding fear of success:

1. Fill your life with love.

Begin by loving yourself. All significant achievement begins with accepting yourself where you are right now, with what you have. You must be real. From there, you get the strength to go on by affirming your belief in yourself, and then surrounding yourself with love and positive thoughts. Success can only begin to happen within the positive cocoon of love. Love heals. It inspires. It comforts. Learn to love yourself. Self-doubt, self-denial, and self-despair are often residuals of self-hatred. By loving yourself unconditionally, you feel a sense of liberation that allows you to share your gift of love with others.

2. Build supportive relationships.

Surround yourself with people who care about your well-being. Supportive relationships are a great source of guidance and comfort. They teach nurturing and provide a good foundation for you to build on. Avoid those who offer toxic love. There's a huge difference between supportive people who understand you and are committed to you, and those who give you toxic love.

Toxic love comes from friends and family members who say they want you to succeed, but who actually want to drag you down with them. They are people who cannot stand to see others succeed around them. How many times have you shared a bit of good news with a friend or family member only to have them say, "That won't last. You may have been lucky once, but it will change," or, "You always screw it up in the end, don't you?" You need to know how to recognize toxic love and keep it from hurting you.

3. Respect yourself, and others will respect you.

Make integrity your constant companion. Self-respect is the next key step. If you count yourself as nothing, no matter where you are on the journey, everyone around you will do the same. It is essential to hold yourself to the highest standards of integrity, to demand it of yourself and of those around you. You will be astonished to see what a difference that will make in your life immediately. As soon as you conduct yourself with integrity, people will start to treat you differently and to raise their estimation of you accordingly.

4. Have a plan for your life—and a plan B.

We are meant to be resilient. Life, like cuts and bruises, is self-healing and renewing. Sometimes that means finding a new path when an old one has been closed to you. Understanding the difference between temporary setbacks and life-changing roadblocks is a key lesson you need to learn from life.

Developing a plan allows you to set realistic goals and take control of the direction you want your life to go in. It forces you to visualize where you want your life to take you. It gives you the freedom to choose the road that will bring you the most happiness and contentment. Developing a plan and having the discipline to carry it out are your keys to success.

Many people spend a tremendous amount of time worrying about things they have no control over. Often decisions are made or things happen that affect you but you have no direct input or influence over those decisions or actions. Therefore, it is important to have a fallback plan. Always remember that anything can happen that might thwart your plans, and if it can, it often will. However, you can control your own destiny. Be prepared for a setback, yet recognize that it will only be a bump in the road on your way to greatness.

5. Work passionately and to the limits of your ability.

Take Action. Life rewards action. Personal success requires acting on your plan. To have a plan without taking action on it is like having an automobile with no fuel. Purposeful action results in accomplishment. Joy and personal satisfaction are the fruits of personal achievement. Our relationship to the world is often established in the world of work. You must find your own positive role in the workplace and fill it as best you can. The positive energy you put into your work will always come back to you in surprising and helpful ways.

6. Embrace obstacles.

There is good news concealed in every setback. What is the good news concealed in each setback you face? What are the opportunities that every obstacle represents? You may be inclined to bemoan the bad news that comes your way. Do you look up at the heavens and say, "Why me?" But often within that apparently bad news is an important lesson, a way forward to a new triumph, or a way to grow. The obstacles you face, the challenges you are confronted with, can be some of your best teachers. Each time you come face-to-face with a difficult, seemingly impossible situation, consider it a lesson in disguise. Use these times to your advantage. From them you

will learn patience, tolerance, perseverance, and
even creativity.

7. Don't sell yourself short.

Believe in yourself and your ability to achieve success
in life. You are capable of accomplishing much more
than you can ever imagine. When you underestimate
your potential, you confine yourself to a life of
mediocrity. Prepare yourself for the life you want.
The rewards can be staggering.

8. Manage change gracefully.

Know that change is inevitable. When unwanted or
unexpected change happens, it can be uncomfortable
and even disruptive. Change can be scary. When you
resist change, you may sabotage your own chance for
personal growth and self-awareness. To resist is futile;
change will happen anyway. Therefore, you should
grab a hold of the wisdom gained from any and all
change and use it for the opportunities it may present.
Accepting change willingly and with flexibility allows
you to open your mind to new possibilities.

9. Continually challenge yourself.

Always be willing to step up your efforts and take
it to the next level. It is often scary to venture into
unchartered territory, but the old adage "Nothing
ventured, nothing gained" has merit. Take the next
step. Empower yourself with a confident, positive
attitude. In so doing, you will be encouraged to

accomplish much more, to achieve greatness, and to stand above the crowd.

10. Find out what makes you happy, then go for it.
You are often so busy in your world of ceaseless activity, that you seldom take time for the things you enjoy. Slow down! Take time to ensure that you have a healthy balance of work, family and play. This will give you peace of mind and a lot less stress.

Should I Fit In or Opt Out?

Unfortunately it is difficult to be a female in a male-dominated society. Women are pressured to fit into a number of stereotypes that create stress and conflict as they try to maneuver through all of the traditional roles that are assigned to them. Having ambitions beyond these traditionally assigned roles are often criticized as being selfish.

As women, we are most often thought of as the housekeepers, the cooks, the caretakers. Even today in education and the world of work, women are encouraged to enter professions that are typically thought of as female occupations such as teachers, nurses and social workers. These are positions that pay less and often those where there is no clear career path to higher salaries and more responsibility. The many stereotypes that women are confronted with often cause them to suffer immense inner turmoil.

Most women spend a great deal of time trying to fit in. You want to be liked or accepted. Peer pressure is as real in your adult life as it was when you were children and teens.

Even as adults, what you wear, how you speak, your behavior, is always under scrutiny. You are always being judged by one superficial standard or another. As social beings you all want to be accepted. The desire to fit in is natural. You don't want to be considered a misfit or an outsider. So, it often becomes easier to conform to someone else's definition of who you should be and how you should act.

I once worked in an office where every Wednesday after work a group of my coworkers would head to the local bar. This was "hump" night and what better way to celebrate having made it halfway through the work week than to celebrate with cocktails, fried chicken wings and an endless evening of line dancing. They would always encourage me to come along. I didn't want to appear unfriendly or standoffish, but I never really wanted to go. Yet I worried that they would not consider me a part of the team or that perhaps they would see me as aloof. I knew that if I went to the bar I would be miserable all evening. Faced with a dilemma of whether to go to the bar or go home was very disconcerting. But, being true to myself and my values, I eventually opted not to go and was very comfortable with that decision.

This is a common dilemma that you will face at times, and it is especially true for women. The pressure to conform can come from many directions. Often, though, it comes from the men in your life. On the one hand, men feel you ought to stay in your lane, and they are more than ready to run you over if you don't. On the other hand, they are quick to point out that you can't possibly measure up because there are too many things pulling at your time. Consequently, too often, you end up conforming to the demands and pressures that are imposed by others.

The problem with conformity is that it inhibits your freedom to be your "true self." As a woman, you spend a lot of time consumed with others' thoughts about you in terms of your roles and responsibilities. You are concerned about how you look, how you talk, what you wear or how you should behave. You tiptoe around people's feelings because you want everyone to be happy and to like you. You devote so much time and energy to trying to fit in that you are distracted from your own desires and aspirations.

But real success comes from knowing yourself. When you know yourself, you are inspired to stay true to your own core values. By knowing yourself, you enrich the culture of an organization and bring wise and diverse perspective to the workplace. For those aspiring to move up in an organization, your authentic self enhances your executive presence at work by garnering respect and confidence from others. It contributes to your own self-worth by giving you the freedom to be honest and forthright in your communications.

What's a Woman to Do?

Bringing your authentic self to the workplace is essential for leadership success. The most important asset you can bring to your leadership is to be yourself. When you are yourself, you have consciously made a choice to show up and be real. There is cohesion between how you feel, think and act. You exude confidence and create a reputation that is built on honesty and credibility. You garner the respect of others. The culture of the workplace is enhanced by your contribution.

How Do I Discover My True Self?

Being your true "authentic" self involves knowing what you believe in and holding true to those beliefs. These are your core values. And in exercising your core values you feel free to say and do those things you believe in. You are not overly concerned with what others think about you or how they will judge you. You have learned to manage your insecurities.

Some steps in discovering your true self might include these:

1. Find your own voice.

You were born with a unique voice. No one else can define who you are or what your purpose in life should be, nor should you rely on others to define these things for you. Finding your voice is a big challenge for most people. Who are you? What are you passionate about? How do you express your passion and your purpose to others? Through introspection and experience you will eventually be able to answer these questions.

Your ideas, feelings and thoughts are uniquely yours. The process of delving into the things that you are passionate about is an exercise in self-awareness that gets you excited and energized. It is through this process that you discover your own truth. It is a process of self-discovery.

Once you've found your voice, continue to develop it. Finding your voice is a quest that may never end. Through experience and continued learning you may find that your voice is continually evolving.

2. Embrace your imperfections.

No one is perfect. You can't be perfect all the time even though some may expect you to be. Being imperfect creatures, we all have flaws; some are just more obvious than others. Your flaws may include being a pessimist, being quirky or being easy to anger. Even so, you need to accept who you are. Don't waste your time trying to be perfect. Instead strive for excellence. Be it with friends, family or in the board-room, always bring your best self to the game.

3. Know what you want.

It is not easy to know what you want. A lot of people live their lives having no clue what they want. They usually follow the American Dream without a second thought, just because that's what's expected of them. That's why the process of discovery can bring you much promise and enlightenment.

4. Be courageous.

Speak your purpose, but always remember to be judicious with your words. Everything that can be said doesn't need to be.

Don't be afraid to take risks or to make mistakes. If you fail at something, use it as a teaching moment. After all, recovering from a mistake or mishap takes effort and it builds resilience, and resilience builds confidence.

5. Dare to be selfish.

Being selfish goes against the grain of everything you've been taught. Yet you can't focus on exactly what you want if you're constantly trying to make others happy. You have to put yourself first because if you don't, no one else will. Don't feel bad for being selfish.

6. Forgive yourself.

Let go of unnecessary baggage that holds you back. Stay focused on the present and the future you want for yourself. Forgiveness is a tool that allows you to accept the past, acknowledge your mistakes, and then move forward. It's your life. Prepare to live it the way you want!

Human beings are naturally social creatures. Socializing and interacting with others usually makes us feel good and feel accepted. Gaining acceptance from our family, peers, and colleagues is an important element in determining our happiness. However, don't get caught up in depending on excessive outside approval to boost your self-esteem. The feeling that you are not pleasing others can result in a fear of social rejection from those you so desperately desire approval from.

On the other hand, it is also normal for human beings to seek attention and praise to validate their successes and achievements. It is okay to want to look good by sharing your successes with others, though don't go overboard. Too much focus on impressing others can be viewed as egotistical.

the checklist

∧

Challenges ... as a leader, you will encounter them on a daily basis. With courage, you will be able to accomplish almost anything ... and forgive yourself when you make a mistake. It will happen.

chapter 3

Purpose ... Follow Your Quest

The only true gift is a portion of yourself.

— Ralph Waldo Emerson, poet

Y ou tell yourself:

I am not supposed to be here.

I am not worthy.

I am not good enough to sit in the boardroom.

I do not have the right skills or talent.

I am in my place; this is my space.

The door is shut, and I am not welcome.

And so, you hide out and try not to be noticed.

The fact that you are uncomfortable being in a place or among certain people is because you don't yet understand your purpose. A sense of purpose guides you and instills within you a sense of confidence. It encourages you to venture out of your tiny space—your comfort zone—and explore opportunity. It gives you the room you need to grow and to exercise your talents and abilities.

> Sorry ... am I supposed to be here?

At one time or another all of you have had that gnawing feeling that something was missing in your life. That you were supposed to be doing more and making a difference in the world. But often you are afraid to venture outside of your comfort zone to experience new things. At other times, you are just not sure what you should be doing with your life. You feel empty and lack a clear direction. These are not uncommon feelings, but it can leave you unsure and searching to find that perfect thing that connects you to your purpose in life.

Where one falls short is the looking part—trying to find purpose. You feel disjointed, as if the pieces of the puzzle aren't quite fitting together. It's like putting on your fanciest outfit, going to a fancy event, and feeling uncomfortable all night because you're concerned that your dress is too tight.

The good news is that purpose is not to be found; it is to be discovered. As you move through your life's journey, you have to be open to the fact that one day your purpose will reveal itself to you. If you are always looking, you never fully engage in those things that you are passionate about. You are in a constant state of turmoil because there is so much clutter in your life, and it makes it difficult to see your way clear to doing the things that are most satisfying to you. And so your purpose often remains elusive.

But don't despair. Very few people really know what they want to do with their lives. On occasion, you may run across people who knew what they wanted to do with their lives early on and they go about planning and preparing for the day when they will realize their dreams. But this type of knowledge is rare. Instead, most people really don't have a clue as to what they want to do. They are constantly in search of that one perfect thing that will bring them true happiness and fulfillment. Many times people may even change their minds several times along the way.

Personally I have thought about or pursued at least five different career paths since my early college years. Truth be told, I am not doing any of those things that I planned early on. However, one or two of them I did use as stepping stones to other positions, while others were just choices that were made out of expedience, lack of knowledge, or that looked attractive while I was searching.

> Leadership is about making out of life a series of stepping stones even though we often encounter a number of stumbling blocks along the way.

But the journey itself turned out to be very useful and even insightful. I realized that my purpose was not necessarily tied to my job or to my possessions. I came to understand that the turmoil that I was experiencing internally had more to do with not having found my true passion. I realized that what I was doing to make ends meet, my job, was not filling the empty void that existed within me. As I began to look at the things in my life that I could control, I began to focus on those that made me want to get up each morning. I realized some things that I was truly passionate about, the things in which I found true gratification and even got excited about. Along the way, I also found out what I really didn't want to do.

Although I still consider myself to be a "work in progress," after a while, it finally dawned on me. I realized one important fact: the purpose of life is very simple. Rather than spending a lifetime searching for the right answer to suddenly surface, just know that **YOUR** purpose is for you to grow into the very best person that you can be. Everything else will flow from this knowledge.

A speech I once gave to a group of women who were being honored gave me an opportunity to share with them my thoughts about living a purposeful life. It went something like this:

The Purpose of Life Is for You to Grow Into the Very Best Person that You Can Be

Today we will honor those among us who have done some pretty remarkable things, and who have worked tirelessly to make their organizations, the community and the region a better place. They have exceeded all expectations and it is these remarkable women whose actions we will recognize and whose lives we will celebrate today.

But this is not a competition. Rather, it is an opportunity to show "exemplars" among us; those who best model the qualities embraced by the YWCA Women of Distinction Awards.

These women have learned to live. They are living with purpose.

I want to take just a few minutes to talk about some of the qualities of those who understand and demonstrate on a daily basis that they are striving to live a purposeful life.

I am going to talk about four of these qualities today.

Leadership:

Women have a natural ability to lead. Ralph Waldo Emerson once said, "The only true gift is a portion of yourself."

With this quote in mind, leadership requires you to:

- Commit yourself to make a difference in the world.
- Be a constant source of encouragement to others.
- Recognize that when you invest in others you help yourself.

When I think of leadership, I'm reminded of a little poem that I came across recently. It's from "A Bag of Tools" by R.E. Sharpe and it goes like this:

Isn't it strange that princes and kings, and clowns that caper in sawdust rings, and common people like you and me are builders of eternity? Each is given a bag of tools, a shapeless mass, a book of rules, and each must make, ere life is flown, a stumbling block or a stepping stone.

Leadership is about making out of life a series of stepping stones even though we often encounter a number of stumbling blocks along the way.

Integrity:

In a world where there is so much corporate scandal and government corruption, and at a time when it is so much easier to go along, just to get along, we need credible people in leadership positions more than ever. As people with integrity, whose credibility is never in question, you have to be willing to:

- Do what's right—*not what's easiest or expedient.*

- Be controlled by values—*not by your moods.*

- Look for solutions—*not excuses.*

- Persevere when challenged—*don't just quit.*

- Rely on internal motivation—*not external motivation.* In other words, don't look for recognition. Just look to do the right thing.

- Say what you mean—*mean what you say.* Words and actions should always agree.

- Make choices that add up to success (no matter how small or incremental)—*don't make choices that you suspect or know will lead to ultimate failure.*

Vision:

A young man that I met a few years ago, Victor Woods, once said, "Eyesight is what you see in front of you. Vision is what you see down the road."

- Find out what makes you happy—then go for it.

- Develop a plan for your life. When you have a plan, you're in control—you're in the driver's seat.

- Have a "Plan B (and sometimes a C)"—it is not a matter of if something will go awry, but when.

- Remember, there is always someone out there who is worse off than you—always.
- Stay focused—never lose sight of the goal.

Excellence:

- Don't sell yourself short. Have confidence in your ultimate success.
- Always be willing to take it to the next level. Don't settle for "good enough."
- Find and explore your source of inner peace. For you, what makes life worth living? How do you find contentment in life?
- Life rewards action. Like the Nike slogan: Just do it! Don't procrastinate.

You have the opportunity to be leaders and to make the world a better place because you've been here. Live life to its fullest! LIVE:

Leadership	Be a beacon of light for yourself and others.
Integrity	Always do what is right, honest and fair.
Vision	Know that you can achieve whatever you believe—whatever you're passionate enough about.
Excellence	Strive for superiority—for greatness.

Live with leadership, integrity, vision, and excellence as your guiding principles and you won't go wrong.

How Will I Know I Am Living with Purpose?

When I think about why I am here—my purpose, it is not hard to recall examples from my work that really resonate and remind me why I do what I am passionate about. A philosophy that we have adopted at Edgewater highlights how our organization functions. A recent example came to mind as I was working on the manuscript for *The Unapologetic Woman*. The following is from a speech I gave at a fundraiser:

> *Our philosophy at Edgewater Systems is that we don't believe in "this is as good as it gets." In fact, we believe that as good as it gets can get even better.*
>
> *We don't believe that mental illness or addiction is a dead-end street. We believe there is a path to recovery and balance to life.*
>
> *I'm often asked, "Why do you do this work?" My answer is usually the same. "I like helping to change people's lives." But, what's even better is actually being able to see the change.*
>
> *Once I was in the grocery store and a woman stopped me. She asked, "You're Dr. Hughes, right? You work at Edgewater Systems, don't you?" I hesitated for just a moment, not knowing what she had in mind, then I responded, "Yes."*
>
> *She started talking to me about her son, Eric, and pointed toward him. She related to me how Eric, then a sophomore in high school, had been kicked out of public school because of behavior problems.*
>
> *I turned and looked over at Eric. He was a big guy … about 6'2" and a good 185 pounds. As I looked at him, I thought to myself that he probably*

*came across as very intimidating to his teachers. She
told me how getting help at Edgewater had made such
a difference. After being registered for our services and
completing a program of therapy and behavior modification, he was able to get back into high school
and graduated shortly thereafter.*

*It's nice to say you work someplace that helps
people. It's nicer when you see those positive changes
happening.*

*Think about it. Eric's mother thought that his
behavior and lack of control was as good as it gets.
At Edgewater, we made as good as it gets even better
for Eric, his mom, and his teachers.*

*And most of all, we made "as good as it gets"
better for Eric's future.*

Purpose—here's what you need to consider. You exist
on earth for an indeterminate period of time. No one has
any idea just how much time. During your time here, you
engage in all kinds of activities. Some of these activities are
inconsequential and some are very important. The inconsequential things are often those things you do to fill time.
The important things are things that help you to discover
and fulfill your purpose. These are the things that fulfill
your passions and give your life meaning.

Work Passionately and to the Limits of Your Ability

"A woman should only appear in the paper when she's
born, she's married and when she dies." Ava Richards relates this belief that her family taught her growing up.

"It made it a challenge to take a stand," she says quietly, with what I'm fast learning is her characteristic modesty. And needless to say, for a woman who has become editor-in-chief of the family-run *The Vanguard*, a champion of underrepresented voices, alternate points of view, and stories not covered by the national media, it has been a challenging journey through life. She has agreed to speak with me about her passion—her life's work.

Ava and I both carry the burden and the excitement of running an organization whose existence is not guaranteed. Edgewater Systems depends on steady reimbursement from insurance companies, and renewals of grants and contracts. *The Vanguard* depends on its readers and advertising revenue. For both of us, there are wakeful nights and days when we're not sure it's all going to work out. We worry because so many people depend on our organizations for their livelihood, and for their own personal sense of safety and sanity. Yet neither of us could imagine doing anything else.

How did we get to where we are, passionately committed to a workplace and a career? Ava and Michael Richards founded *The Vanguard* many years ago to publish the stories that weren't being covered by mainstream media. I began my work in the mental health industry emptying bedpans in a state psychiatric hospital. I was 17.

I hated the job. The hours were long, the pay was bad, and the work was horrible. Once, when I had been late for work a few days in a row, my supervisor asked me what my problem was. "I'm angry," I started to explain. "You're always angry," came the reply.

That comment caught me by surprise. I started to think about it. Was I always angry? I didn't think of myself as that way. Was that how I seemed to other people? Why was I coming across that way?

Suddenly, I wanted to change. My long, slow turnaround began at that moment. It was the moment I decided to take control of my life and stop thinking of myself as a victim. It was the moment that I started to think about getting an education so that I wouldn't always have to be changing bedpans. It was the moment I realized that the power lay within me to change my circumstances. No one else was going to do it.

For Ava, the journey began with her father, a driven man who wanted a son, and instead got three daughters.

> He called us Nuisance Numbers One, Two, and Three. The effect on us was to make us unsure of ourselves.

I, too, know what it is like to grow up in a household with a father who didn't understand the harmful effect of his words. My father was constantly criticizing us, telling us we would fail, and saying "I told you so," when we did.

> Because I didn't have to earn a living, there was a lot of pressure on me to find out what really mattered. I couldn't just go out and earn a wage. It wouldn't have been significant enough.

> More pressure, she smiles ruefully. It was a burden that a lot of people would love to have, but it did have a double edge to it. And so I did various different things, but I didn't follow any particular path. You could say I was searching for my role in life.

In the end, it was having children that helped Ava find herself and her way in life.

> Having kids was important for me, because it gave me a sense of priorities. This was hugely liberating for me. Everyone talks about how little time you have when the children are born, but it helped me structure my life. Time was more precious, so I used it better.

Then came *The Vanguard*, and an opportunity for Ava to put the organizing skills she had learned raising children to use in the workplace.

> I was involved in the early years when it was a bootstrap kind of thing. We'd have salons in our house to discuss the issues we thought were important.

From the start, *The Vanguard* sought to bring to light stories that were not receiving attention in the national press.

> As the number of media outlets get smaller and smaller, concentrated in a few large corporations, alternate voices are getting harder and harder to hear. The (second) Iraq war is a good example. The mainstream press was so ready to get embedded with the troops, that they were sounding the drumbeat for war even before it started. There was no real discussion of the pros and the cons.

Today, the newspaper and all it represents have become Ava's life's work. The family's personal fortunes are tied to the success or failure of the newspaper, a frequently frightening proposition in an era of declining subscriptions and ad revenues throughout the industry.

When I fell into this job of editor-in-chief, I had a recurring dream that I was the captain of the boat, but I didn't know what to do. I had a crew, but I didn't know what to do. Someone actually has to be the captain, or the boat can't be run smoothly and successfully.

> When I started talking to people about selling **The Vanguard**, I realized that I would be compromising our independence and our ability to take a stance.

My husband Michael, who was the first editor, was a workaholic. Eventually, he got burned out and took a sabbatical. We weren't sure what to do. Should we sell the newspaper? I had invested a lot of the family money in it. At that point, I said, "Give it to me and I'll at least get my money back." This is a good thing and it deserves to survive. I wanted to nurture it and then send it off to someone else.

But when I started talking to people about selling **The Vanguard**, I realized that I would be compromising our independence and our ability to take a stance. At the time, I didn't know how to be a publisher or an editor, but this was something I cared about, and it was hemorrhaging money! So I stepped in to become editor and to save the business.

It hasn't been an easy path of discovery for Ava.

> It's taken me a long time to take ownership of the company. It's taken me a long time to feel I could step up to the editor-in-chief role. I'm loyal and felt strongly about supporting the people who had done the work before I got here. There had to be a gradual process of turnover. Now it's almost all a new crew. In a way, if I'd been clearer and more ruthless, it might have been better. I see a lot better in hindsight!

And did that early pressure from her father help her in the process of learning to run the newspaper? Ava says,

> I recently spoke with him at a family gathering. He asked me what I had learned from him. I thought about it and told him that all you can do as a leader is get the best information, make the best decisions and take responsibility for what happens after. That's what I learned from my father.

> It hasn't been easy. It's a tough business. There isn't another title that's independent and makes money. **The Vanguard** is an independent media company. We believe that personal growth is the key to social change. Our mission is to seek out and illuminate people who want to make the world change.

As I talked with Ava in *The Vanguard* offices on a cold winter day in Wisconsin, I was constantly learning from this woman who has become the voice of millions of people who don't have a voice. Not only has Ava learned how to run a newspaper, she has also learned wisdom.

I asked her to talk about work, and what it means to her.

> My parents had a healthy respect for all kinds of work, Ava muses. There was nothing that was demeaning or unworthy of respect. Work deserves respect.

And what advice does she have for people just beginning in the workplace?

> A couple of things ... first, you're going to be afraid at times, Ava says. Fear is our companion in the world; you have to learn to deal with it. If you take fear to mean stop, you are not going to get anywhere.

> Second, it's not all about you. It's about what needs to happen. I get freaked out and overwhelmed on a regular basis. Then, I take a deep breath and remember that it's not about me, but it's about what I'm in service to. All you can do is do your best. Know to stop and take a breath and see what's next. Anyone who says they've got it all mapped out is bogus. Life doesn't work that way.

I look out Ava's window and see snowflakes begin to fall in the fading light of the winter afternoon. I ask her if she's happy about where she's ended up, especially considering that she more or less fell into editing *The Vanguard*, whereas for me it was a long, slow climb through education to where I am today.

Ava doesn't hesitate.

> I love what I do. I have a bouquet of activities that I engage in. But the form didn't really matter. It matters a lot more how you do it. That's where the passion comes in—doing whatever you are doing wholeheartedly. People who are successful are so because of how much of themselves they are willing to put out into the world. My advice is just get over yourself and do it.

Ava concludes our interview with a story.

> I heard a woman speak the other day, and she moved me to do something I have never done before. I've agreed to fast with her! Her name is Delia Robertson.

> Delia Robertson is a shrimp fisherwoman from the Gulf of Mexico with five kids. She is a Vietnam vet. She didn't graduate from high school. She started noticing that something bad was happening to the dolphins and shrimp. She educated herself about pollution and started speaking out about it. She took on some very powerful business interests who were polluting the Gulf.

> She was unreasonable. She wouldn't be quiet, and wouldn't take "no" for an answer. That's what the world needs now: more unreasonable women. Her message was so powerful for me that when she called on her audience to fast, I had to join her. So I'm fasting.

It's people like that that we need to support with
the newspaper; people who can change your life
with a message. They are beacons of hope who
inspire other people who think the same way.

I'm very optimistic, Ava says. But optimism is a
really practical choice, for me. It isn't automatic.
I do believe that people are doing their best at
any given time.

In the end, when you allow others to stifle your dreams
and your abilities, they can erode your confidence. In such
an environment, it's easy to begin to think that you are not
worthy or good enough. Thankfully Ava decided those things
didn't matter. The culture that she grew up in and the negative
words of others could not deter her passions. From becoming
a mother and "falling into a job," she discovered her purpose
of being a voice for those whose voices go unheard by shining
a light on issues that many would chose to ignore.

The Quest to Discover Your Purpose

Some days you may spend hours feeling aimless, unsure of
yourself, passionless. You may feel that there's something
deeper you should be a part of, that you have an ethereal
calling that you have not yet
uncovered. You are frustrated
because you can't get a handle
on it. It is ever so elusive.

> When you discover and follow
> your purpose, it will change your
> life for the better and enrich the
> lives of so many more.

Yet, it is your experiences
in life that helps you to discover your purpose, your values.
Your experiences define the things that motivate you, that

keep you going. Your experiences highlight the things that attract and hold your attention, that dominate your thoughts that appeal to your instinctual sense of being. Your passions evolve from your experiences. And your purpose—your calling—evolves from your passions.

Many people mistakenly believe that their success and their worth are measured by their prestigious job, their big house, or their material possessions. Many people spend much of their lives doing jobs or activities that they may not truly believe in or feel motivated by. Because life is finite, much of this is wasted time or time fillers that cause us to miss out on potential opportunities. It can also lead to a tremendous amount of stress.

But it is through personal reflection and your heart that you are able to discover your true purpose. Many people discover their purpose from their chosen career path or profession. Others discover their purpose in the way they have come to express themselves through their personal creativity or individuality. Either way, your life's purpose flows from your unwavering fidelity to your values, to those things that you are passionate about.

The following are a few methods you can employ to help you discover your purpose:

1. Look back at your life.

What things did you enjoy doing? What things happened in your past that you would not want to repeat? By looking back at your past experiences, you can begin to identify those things that added value to your life and those things you should avoid. A retrospective look at your life will help you to identify your passions and your competencies. It will give you a good place to start as you plan your future.

2. Eradicate yourself of your inner demons.

Discovering your purpose takes courage. Delving into the deeper essence of who you are with objectivity and honesty can invoke fears that can stop you in your tracks. Your beliefs about who you are and why you are that way can either limit you or invoke excitement. Either way, it is a very personal journey inside your physical, emotional and psychological self that allows you to see who you really are. If there is emotional baggage that is blocking your ability to thrive, you can begin to acknowledge it and deal with it. You can then put your full effort into going for your passion.

3. Get busy!

For many there is a gap between who you feel you are and the life that you are leading. The failure to make the connection leaves you with a void of uncertainty. Within that void lies missed opportunity and a major source of stress. To make the pieces fit, it is imperative that you tie your actions to those things that you get excited about. When you have discovered your purpose , you find that you feel better about yourself and that your life and your work has meaning. You are motivated to do things that help other people. Your actions become part of a greater personal and social mission.

the ∧ **checklist**

Simply put, when you discover and follow your purpose, it will change your life for the better and enrich the lives of so many more.

chapter 4

Women:
Our Own Worst
Enemies

Professional jealousy, insecurity and herd mentality
can easily impede your progress in an organization.
— Carol Orsag Madigan, author

Imagine yourself faced with a problem that won't go away. A problem that didn't even have a name until just a few years ago. The problem keeps growing, threatening to destroy your workplace. If not resolved, you may lose your job, or key individuals will quit, or the word will spread that no one who is in her right mind wants to work with your team.

The problem mushrooms. You are criticized for not dealing with the hostility and tension within your team. Everything that you learned in your post-degree classes seems for naught—nothing ever addressed the issues you are experiencing in the types of covert activities when women work with other women. Your self-doubts are building; you begin to feel paranoid. Is someone trying to cut your job out from under you?

One day, after a series of events, everything unravels. The woman you had mentored the past year had given incorrect information to others, including the CEO. Folders and files have mysteriously disappeared from your computer. What you thought was a perfect workplace life has nothing that is perfect in it.

You are now plagued by recurring nightmares, nightmares that are so horrible that you don't want to remember anything about them in the morning. When you wake, you are exhausted. You've concluded that the business world is the pits and wonder why you ever left your first love of working with preschoolers.

You feel like an emotional and physical wreck. You seek professional help, yet nothing works. Your family and friends are worried. So are you.

You are not alone. Others echo your experiences and are revealed in Judith Briles' book, *Stabotage: How to Deal with the Pit Bulls, Skunks, Snakes, Scorpions & Slugs in the Health Care Workplace.* Thousands have reported the same phenomenon in their workplaces. The phrase, "Nurses eat their young," has been repeated for eons in health care. According to Briles, "It's not just nurses, it's women in general who eat their young."

Sorry ... Did You Mean Me?

Today's women are caught up in a Catch-22. They are not raised to be confrontational, rather societal expectations are that women should conform and be ladylike at all times. They are supposed to be nurturers and intermediaries. They should be honest and exhibit emotional composure and restraint. This line of thinking holds that women should be slow to anger and that they should never be aggressive.

But these expectations are unrealistic. Every human being occasionally has feelings of anger, jealousy, shame, sadness, and fear. Because they are expected to remain composed, women often have no real outlet for a lot of these emotions. When women experience conflict, to react by becoming verbally or physically aggressive is frowned upon. Aggressive behavior is typically ascribed to men. They are considered natural competitors and protectors of our honor—just leave everything to them. Women are therefore left to internalize these emotions that they are prohibited from displaying publicly. Subsequently, many of them adopt a passive-aggressive response that is most often directed toward other women and can be personally harmful, but after all, lashing out at other women is usually safer.

As I have advanced in my career, I've frequently encountered situations where my female colleagues have tried to undermine me. With each promotion or more responsible position, the attacks became more venomous and more blatant. I was always shocked by the animosity and hatred. It was particularly disturbing and unexpected considering that some of my childhood mentors had been women. Once an overweight female colleague, after observing what was going on, said to me, "I don't have those problems. I'm matronly." I thought, "What an indictment of women and their poor behavior!"

What I have discovered in my career is that women—generally as a group—don't think very highly of themselves. That's because most of us mistakenly believe that our happiness depends on outside circumstances. We believe that if we solve our problems, improve our relationships, or achieve success, we will find happiness and contentment. But our daily struggles tell us that these things are fleeting. On any given day, at any given time, we can interact with someone, or something, which can create a whole new problem for us and, thus, upset the balance in our daily routines. As a result, we may become upset or angry—so much so that often we can think of nothing else but the situation causing these feelings of agitation. We allow ourselves to become consumed with anger, or jealousy, or worry, or some other unhealthy emotion. Unfortunately, when we allow anger, stress, conditions, and desires to consume us, we surrender control of our lives to someone or to something else. We lash out to relieve the tension.

If you're anything like me, you might ask yourself in one of your down moments, "Why do people dislike me so much? Why do they judge me so harshly?" You tell yourself, "They don't like the way I look, what I wear, how I talk." You think to yourself, "I can't win." And, you begin to wonder, "What am I doing wrong?"

The answer is absolutely nothing! The problem is not you, it's them. Their own insecurities have gotten in the way. Their flawed thinking has caused them to doubt their own abilities and to feel you are out to take something away from them such as their man, their social standing, or their job. They may begin to label you as arrogant, aloof or snotty. They are the naysayers and detractors. You need only understand that this is as much a reflection of how they view themselves as it is of their view of you. They simply have not recognized that you have decided to "stand in your power."

But don't allow yourself to be sidetracked. Others will see you as the amazing and talented individual that you are. And this is where you should direct your efforts. Your job is not to give in to the insecurities of the few. Instead, your job, indeed, your obligation is to continue to live up to your purpose, and be an example of how everyone should continue to strive to be her very best—kind, supportive, giving human beings.

Yet, many of you have difficulty accepting just how powerful you are. You have trouble ridding yourself of the nagging baggage of insecurity that is often caused by the ill intent of others. It can be the constant undermining of your efforts in the form of backbiting, malicious gossip and, yes, even sabotage. Those who engage in this activity are like crabs. They haven't learned what it takes to get to the top of the barrel.

Will We Ever Learn the Secret to Getting to the Top?

Look into the barrel. See them in there: scuttling about, bumping into each other, claws clicking. As one tries to rise, the others prevent it, more out of thoughtlessness than on purpose.

This is called the *Crabs in the Barrel Syndrome*.

I can't recall where I first heard the term, and can only guess at the origins of the phrase. I do know that I have heard the "crabs in the barrel" psychology described quite often, in both my professional experience and in social situations. It is a true psychological phenomenon that often has had devastating effects on the mental, emotional and psychological well-being of many.

I strongly suspect the term has its source in a cultural phenomenon, since I've heard it used most often in the African American community. "Crabs in the Barrel" could be rooted in the early experiences of slavery, when some slaves felt it was to their benefit to spy on other slaves for the "masters," and to gain preferential treatment in this way.

> If only everyone could realize how much satisfaction exists in helping others reach their goals.

In fact, on the website of the National Association of Juneteenth Lineage Inc., there is an accurate description of the "crabs in the barrel" mentality. It relates the way in which these crustaceans crawl all over one another "fighting for territory" and "pulling each other down" with the result that none of the crabs ever reach the top of the barrel.

"Must we continue to be like those 'crabs in the barrel'?" the writer asks. "Is this how the 'masters' got the idea that we, as a people, would never do anything to change our condition, but will rather allow this behavior to continue until the end of time?"

The syndrome is present, unfortunately, in more than just African American society. The business world is often fraught with people who, rather than achieve their own success, do all that's in their power to hold others back. In an article entitled "The War Against Office Politics" in an issue of *Controller Newspaper*, author Carol Orsag Madigan writes:

> Even in a healthy corporate culture, political in-
> fighting can be a drain on resources. Where do we
> draw the line between healthy competitive spirit
> and Machiavellian maneuvers?

Madigan goes on to use a story often told by Alberta Lloyd, Vice President of Coleman Management Consultants Inc., that is dead-on about "crabs in the barrel:"

> One crab decides to crawl out. Soon all the other
> crabs start the climb, and the first crab can't get
> anywhere because it keeps catching its claws on
> all the other crabs.

> The business analogy: Professional jealousy, inse-
> curity and herd mentality can easily impede your
> progress in an organization. I may be one of the
> crabs in the barrel that doesn't have any partic-
> ular job objectives. I don't want what you want,
> but I continually pull at you to a point where the
> stress becomes great and you become terribly
> frustrated.

Yikes. Have you ever been caught by a "crab in the barrel"? The saddest thing about a "crabs in the barrel" mentality is not merely the way that it tends to hold back those who seek to achieve higher goals, but also those who do the holding back. Think of the time and energy these people expend in blocking the advancement of others, and how much could be done if all that negative effort was turned into positive effort.

The fact is, the world contains enough happiness, joy and success for all to share in, if only everyone could cooperate with one another, if only everyone could realize how much satisfaction exists in helping others reach their goals.

The author of *Crabs in the Barrel* on the National Association of Juneteenth Lineage Inc. website puts it most effectively: "Rather than pulling one another down, let us begin to lift each other up; lead when we are called upon to lead by the masses, rather than attempting to build up our own egos. When we have become part of an organization seeking to give us knowledge, let us become workers rather than deceivers and destroyers of one another."

Working in an environment filled with "crabs" can be emotionally exhausting, and so too can the feeling of being constantly undermined by other women.

Why Do Women Undermine Other Women?

They're referred to as she-devils, bitches, witches, backstabbers, saboteurs, and other unflattering terms. These are the women who undermine other women. Examples can be seen as early as middle school when two girls start out as friends. One girl has a boyfriend. The boyfriend ends up with the other girl but the girl gets blamed and not the guy. Examples like this set the stage for hateful and unhealthy competition between women throughout their lives.

Later as you enter high school and college, the behavior often becomes more intense. The prevailing notion is that women compete, compare, undermine, judge, and berate one another with deliberate intention and little thought. So the underlying question becomes why is it that women as a group have a reputation for not supporting and even going so far as to undermine other women?

University of Ottawa Professor Tracy Vaillancourt has done a fair amount of research on female competitiveness. She has found that generally speaking women often express *indirect* aggression toward other women. The aggressive behavior is a combination of self-promotion, making themselves look more attractive, and "derogation of rivals (being mean spirited toward other women)."

Many scholars believe that girls become used to having their personal boundaries invaded early in life. As a result, they internalize this behavior as being acceptable and so they grow up believing it is okay to treat other women that same way.

> Girls' opinions are often ignored or treated as unimportant.

There is also some thinking that girls are different in a way that makes their parents want to be more protective of them, that there is a special innocence about them that parents want to see kept intact. Conversely, boys are encouraged to explore, to be more assertive, and to show more aggression in sports and in life.

Girls' opinions are often ignored or treated as unimportant. They are often encouraged to have smaller career aspirations than boys, e.g., marry a doctor as opposed to becoming a doctor. Boys are raised to believe that everything they do is golden. Girls are raised to practice restraint and humility in all that they do for fear of being seen as too pushy.

As a result, early in their lives, girls' potential contribution to humanity is devalued by their parents and others. They are told to be more realistic about their dreams. They, therefore, become accustomed to unfair treatment, disparaging comments, and a devaluation of their self-worth.

This early indoctrination follows them. As they move into the workplace, you may hear women speak of other women who have undermined their efforts to move up in the workplace. Often they refer to a female boss who impeded their ability to move up the career ladder. Others speak of women who have managed to crack the proverbial "glass ceiling" then made no effort to help others join their ranks. Women's failure to support other women is frequently cited as one significant reason that there aren't more women at the top in organizations.

Many women's social organizations that purport to exist to foster sisterhood and friendship frequently fall short of their mission. A prevailing notion is that these organizations can appear to nonmembers as an enviable organization to belong to, but for many of its members it can be a den of negativity and cliques, with members who operate with righteous indignation and contempt for their "sisters." Among the things said about women is that they do not extend a hand to each other through mentoring and, more seriously, that they may attempt to sabotage each other through catty behavior and social isolation.

As an adult, I can now look back and see that as the fourth of seven children, positioned firmly in the middle of my siblings, I had a severe case of middle child syndrome. In general, this malady produced in me intense feelings of not amounting to much. I was frequently left feeling that my older siblings got all the accolades and rewards and the younger siblings received all of my parents love. As the middle child, I felt that I got nothing. For instance, I can recall vividly that all of my siblings at one time or another got a brand new sleek looking bike. I got my older sister's hand-me-down clunker and not the sleek new models that my other sisters and brothers got. I got all the hand-me-down clothes, including my brother's jacket that I was forced to wear to school and that caused me a great deal of humiliation because of the teasing I got from my peers. This was the beginning of my low self-esteem period.

This feeling of not amounting to much stayed with me through adolescence and beyond. Many researchers have associated low self-esteem with a number of risk and protective factors. Throughout elementary and middle school I found it very hard to cope with the pressures from school, my peers and society in general. The stress of being expected to achieve good grades, look a certain way and be successful or popular was sometimes overwhelming.

Although I was generally a good student, I felt otherwise—that I was not good at things and that I did not deserve to be loved or supported. Although I had thoughts of a different and better life, I did not have very high aspirations beyond my everyday existence. I soon found that being a good student with hope for a better life was not popular among my peers.

For me, entering middle school was an awkward time. I found it so hard to fit in. I was teased for my hand-me-down clothes. I was teased by all the mean girls. I thought of myself as skinny and I felt ugly. I was bullied because I dared to get good grades and because I dared to practice what I learned in school, namely using deliberate care in my speech by pronouncing my words correctly and using proper grammar.

It was not until I became a young woman that I began to think better of myself. I went to college and got a degree. I worked, sometimes two jobs, while I went to undergraduate and graduate school. I started to earn my own money. I was able to buy "new clothes." And, frequently people would remark about how attractive I was. However, the spirit of the mean girls of my childhood resurfaced and became the dreaded she-devils of my adult life.

These are the women whose nails come out as they try to bond with other like-minded women by putting other women down through malicious gossip, unfair judgment, criticism, and cold treatment. They are mean-spirited and direct their venom toward other women because they have the audacity to be different. And boy, am I different! Words that could have described me at various points in my life include poor, high school dropout, pregnant teen, and divorcee. So too the words educated, CEO, entrepreneur, and author in more recent times. No matter the descriptors, there is always the catty sniping that occurs when the she-devils come out, pitch forks waving, whose mission it is to put other women down.

As women, you've all been there. Like me, you've probably asked yourself "why me?" You have probably asked the same thing of those close to you, trying to put this obvious hatred and dislike into perspective. There is always that one woman who immediately turns into the dreaded ice queen at the very sight of you, despite your having done absolutely nothing to wrong her in any way. In my clinical training and experience, I have come to accept that women are intrinsically insecure, jealous and competitive.

Other examples: you enter a room and immediately know that the group of women sitting at the table in the back are viciously gossiping and maligning you. Or, you attend a cocktail party and happen to walk up to a group of women making derogatory comments about a very attractive acquaintance that just happens to be minding her own business. On a personal level, I can recall the nasty rumors about how I landed in such a high level position. And of course you can guess that it had nothing to do with my years of academic preparation and the skills I had developed throughout my career. The rumor was that I somehow slept my way to the top. Comments like these are hurtful and can literally destroy the faint of heart. Fortunately, today that is not me.

Some have theorized that the understanding of female competitiveness is actually very misleading. You think of this bad behavior as emanating from feelings about the other woman. However, there is much thought and research that points to the fact that the competition is usually within yourself and not with other women. It is about how many women view themselves relative to the ideal of what is prettier, smarter, or better and how it equates to what you see when you look in the mirror. It is an internal emotional battle waging inside some women and compelling them to constantly compare their body image, intellect, and sexuality to what they think is acceptable in society.

How Do You Fix It?

Throughout my life, I have encountered many amazing women. These beautiful, secure and supportive women make it a practice to help other women. These women understand how difficult it is at times for women to get the help they need in corporate America. Former Secretary of State Madeleine Albright once made a somewhat controversial statement when she said, "There's a special place in hell for women who don't help other women."

> Nothing changes until you change.

While I can't speak to where any of you will ultimately land at the end of this life, I can speak to the need for women to stop sniping at each other and band together as allies in this very difficult and challenging world. Women still get the short end of the stick and it can't be changed without a united effort. It is about time that women stop undermining each other and recognize that as a group, women can get further and achieve more by banding together and supporting one another.

Unlike women, men have a special mental code that they have consciously and subconsciously put into practice. Men have "man law," and they do honor it! This well-honed and protected code is rarely violated by any man for fear of being exiled from the "brotherhood." Generally speaking, men have no problem helping other men get their piece of the pie as long as they get theirs. They don't even have to like each other but they work together when it is in their mutual best interest.

Why can't women have their own special code that they use in an effort to advance all women? Why can't women be so organized and protective of their own set of rules and not allow it to be intruded upon by the other gender? This show of harmony can go a long way in sending a message that women are united in their demand for respect, equal treatment and a voice in decisions that impact them.

It's time to focus on cutting each other some slack. Commitment to changing bad habits and making choices that positively impact the quality of life for you and other women is simply that—a choice. Here are some of the things that you can do to begin the process:

- *Make a conscious choice to stop bad-mouthing other women.* Don't participate in hate sessions where women intentionally disparage and pull others down. If you refuse to participate, the conversation will likely stop and others may be more reluctant to initiate such dialogue in your presence.

- *Speak up.* Don't be afraid to be confrontational. You can be confrontational and respectful at the same time. Be courageous in offering an alternative viewpoint. Think about it. Where would the world be if everyone engaged in "group think?"

- *Allow time in your schedule to serve as a mentor to other women.* As women, you have so many demands on your time. Therefore you don't have a lot of free time to help others. But, you have to make time because if you have a successful career, it is likely that some-one helped you to get there, and chances are it was a woman.

- *Recognize that both men and women can serve as mentors.* Seek out mentors from both genders to gain a well-rounded perspective. Some of my best mentors have been men.

- *Regularly collaborate with other women.* Direct them to resources that can benefit them in their work and personal lives. Share information that can benefit them and that can help them to excel.

- *Sponsor and promote other women if you have the opportunity.* If you are in a position to hire or promote women, be sure to look for competent, well-qualified women. When you find them, give them the support, coaching and mentoring to demonstrate and build on their skill sets.

- *Always endeavor to be a positive role model for other women.* You never know who is watching you and how your behavior influences them, especially the younger generation.

- *Build your own support network of strong, secure, independent and caring women.* It may be a challenge, but if you are determined you will find colleagues and friends who are supportive and always have your best interests in mind. Invite them into your personal circle and hold on to them for dear life.

- *Practice reciprocity.* It is rare that anyone achieves much without help from others. Just as someone helped you, be open to helping someone else. Do everything you can to help them succeed. The pie is big enough that everyone can have a slice.

Nothing changes until you change. Understand that you are much stronger and more successful when you work together. This is a personal choice that you can make. It all begins with the power of choice! Be the change you want to see.

Your Own Worst Enemy ... YOU!

On the other hand, too often you get so wound up in your own insecurities that you frequently feel that everyone is out to get you. You are so distracted by the noise created by your own internal turmoil that you lose sight of the present moment. Perhaps your life experiences have caused you to be on the defensive. You unconsciously believe that every action that impacts you in a negative way is intentional or that others are not supportive of your efforts.

Don't be consumed with how others feel or think about you. If you stay focused on the present moment and don't get distracted by the noise, it is easier to see through the clutter in your mind. You begin to understand that many times when someone says or does something harmful, it's not really about you. More often than not, it's about their own pain, fear or confusion. It's about the insecurity that they are feeling or an unmet need that they have. It's not about you!

the checklist

As I have said before, there are some beautiful, secure, intelligent, and supportive women out there. Actively seek them out. Don't ever assume that because she is a "she" that she is your closest friend and ally. Close friends and allies are "earned degrees!" Make the choice to continue to move forward and accomplish great things. There are many women who are willing to help you. These women have come to understand that there is enough joy, happiness and success for all to share in.

chapter 5

Bullying
Is Not Just
Physical

Workplace bullying is often harmful to an organization
because it impedes the organization's growth and success.

We've heard a lot recently about bullying in the classroom, but what about bullying in the boardroom? Yes, bullying is a pressing problem in today's workplace. According to the Workplace Bullying Institute (WBI), 27 percent of the U.S. work force report being bullied at work. That's an estimated 37 million Americans being bullied right now! An additional 21 percent of people have witnessed workplace bullying. In all, 65.6 million Americans have firsthand experience with workplace bullying in some way. That's a lot of bullying that women are confronted with.

In the WBI 2014 National Survey, workplace bullying was defined as repeated mistreatment. The repeated abusive conduct was documented as: threatening, humiliating, intimidating, work sabotage, or verbal abuse. The report indicated that of those bullied, 69 percent of bullies are men; 60 percent of bullied targets are women; and women bullies choose women targets 68 percent of the time.

Dealing with Intimidation and Workplace Bullying

Robin M. Kowalski, professor of psychology at Clemson University and an expert in the field of interpersonal behavior and social anxiety and the author of *Complaining, Teasing and Other Annoying Behaviors*, writes:

> One of the most common reasons for teasing or bullying is to promote social conformity. People do not react favorably to those who stand out from the crowd. Such individuals are treated as outcasts and ridiculed.

At first glance, it's easy to brush off workplace bullying as just the way business is done. After all, haven't you heard such phrases as "It's a dog eat dog world" and "Only the strong survive"? But being driven to succeed and being a bully are two completely different things.

The fact is that workplace bullying is often harmful to an organization because it impedes the organization's growth and success. It also costs organizations dearly in terms of lost productivity, increased use of sick days, and time for management's intervention. For example, WBI estimates that between lost productivity and turnover alone, workplace bullying could cost a Fortune 500 company $24 million each year. Add another $1.4 million for litigation and settlement costs, and this is one problem no company can afford to ignore.

> Being driven to succeed and being a bully are two completely different things.

My first experience with bullying was in my own home as a child growing up. And, the first bully I ever encountered was my father. You see, a bully is nothing more than a person who is habitually cruel, overbearing or intimidating, especially to smaller or weaker people. That is how he was to my mother. He was, at times both verbally and physically abusive. As kids in the household, my brothers, sisters and I suffered the brunt of his cruelty.

It seemed that everyone in the neighborhood knew that ours was not a very happy household And you know that other kids can be so unkind: we were made fun of because of the abuse, but also because we were poor. The kids laughed at our hand-me-down clothes and old worn out shoes. I was embarrassed many days to go to school because of the teasing. But thankfully, I had a first grade teacher, Mrs. Kaufman, who took an interest in me. She helped me to get through each day without feeling so alone and so bad about myself.

The saddest part of this story, is that because my dad was a bully, it created the opportunity for other kids to bully me. I got burned from both ends. Kids who are bullied often grow up and continue to be bullied or become bullies themselves.

Since everyone has the right to work in a safe, healthy, and bully-free workplace, what can employees and leaders do to stop workplace bullying? The key is to follow the three R's.

• Recognize It

Say the word "bully" and most people envision a playground thug threatening the weakest kid around. In the workplace, bullying often looks much different. While screaming, yelling, and cursing at someone certainly constitutes bullying, other lesser-recognized forms of bullying include:

- Belittling employees
- Excluding people from meetings and other activities
- Denying employees the resources or assistance needed to get the job done
- Spreading nasty rumors about people
- Ignoring employees
- Making dismissive remarks
- Dishing out unwarranted blame or criticism

Ultimately, anything that can be construed as an act of intimidation is really a form of bullying. And when people feel intimidated, they can't get their job done effectively. Interestingly, both men and women bully. But the majority of bullying is same-gender harassment, which is a loophole often overlooked in anti-discrimination laws and workplace policies.

• Refuse It

If you feel you're being bullied in any way, simply refuse the attack. In other words, don't engage the person who is bullying you. You have choices. Don't acknowledge the behavior, ignore it. Or, walk away.

Yes, sometimes this is very difficult, especially if someone is yelling at you or pushing your buttons. But engaging with the person in the same manner he or she is attacking you will only spiral the situation out of control. Not engaging the bully and showing that his or her words or actions have no effect usually will result in the bullying person going away.

If the bullying action includes your being ignored or ostracized, you need to take the lead and initiate a conversation with that person. State that you feel you are being ignored and why this behavior is impeding your ability to get the job done. Make sure you focus on the behavior rather than the individual specifically to reduce the chances of that person becoming defensive.

> The only way to curb workplace bullying is to tackle the issue head on.

• Report It

If you cannot handle the bullying situation yourself, you need to talk to someone who can make a difference. Depending on the situation, this could mean talking with your boss, HR manager, or even a manager in another department. Keep going up the chain of command until you find someone who can intervene on your behalf. If no one within your organization seems willing or able to help, you may want to file a complaint against the bully with your industry's professional organization (if you have one). Fortunately, almost anything can be worked out if both parties are open to it. You simply need to find someone to act as a moderator if talking one-on-one with the bully isn't an option.

A Bully-Free Future

With all this said, realize that a leader who is tough or demanding is not necessarily a bully. All bosses have the right and obligation to set and uphold high standards of performance, as long as they exercise fairness, respect, and objectivity in their dealings with subordinates and others. Therefore, to differentiate whether your boss is being a bully or simply being tough, check if you or your co-workers are being singled out in a negative or demeaning way. Bullying is often a personal attack; leading in a firm and focused way is not.

The only way to curb workplace bullying is to tackle the issue head on. The more awareness people have of the topic, and the more prepared they are to deal with it, the more progress companies will make to end the problem once and for all.

Dealing with Unwanted Male Attention

Intimidation in the workplace can take on many forms. For women, the workplace can already be a daunting and unfriendly place. Not only do you have to contend with issues of men not appreciating or respecting you as being equally as competent and deserving, but often you have to put up with unwanted advances or suggestive comments that can create an uncomfortable work environment. This behavior can lead to feelings of intimidation. In the business world, this behavior is referred to as sexual harassment and it can involve unwanted comments, gestures, actions, or attention that is intended to hurt, offend, or intimidate another person, usually a woman. Outside of the world of work, it is referred to as unwanted sexual attention. In any case, the focus of this unwanted and unsolicited behavior is on things like a woman's appearance or body parts.

"My eyes are up here!" is a familiar quote from women in movies and sitcoms as they try to redirect the focus of the guys they are talking to. But isn't this the way women often feel when confronted with the roving eyes of a boss, colleague or co-worker? Having a boss, client or co-worker making comments about how attractive you are or staring at your body can be annoying at best.

Have you ever walked away from a conversation you were having with a guy only to feel his eyes burning a hole in your derriere. You think, "What's the matter with him? Doesn't he know how obvious he is and how inappropriate he's being?" Worse than that, as you walk away you feel a tinge of embarrassment or even humiliation. Is he too stupid to understand that you are not flattered by his unwanted attention? Sometimes it feels as if unwanted attention is the price to be paid for stepping outside your front door.

Men just don't get it! Women don't want that type of attention so they bite their tongues and cringe every time they see them walk through the door. Moreover, being hit on is exhausting.

> Even before a young girl hits puberty, she often has to contend with unwanted advances.

Personally, I enjoy looking good for work or anywhere that I might go. I try to look my best at work, church, a funeral or even the grocery store. I try to look my best all the time.

I won't leave home without my lipstick and a little blush on my cheeks even when I'm not going anywhere of particular importance for fear I might run into someone I know. Personal pride keeps me from ever looking unkempt outside of my home.

Unfortunately from an early age, often even before a young girl hits puberty, she has to contend with unwanted advances. Groping, inappropriate sexually explicit conversation and remarks, and lewd stares can create an untenable environment for a young girl. Sometimes the behavior can take a more egregious turn resulting in actual sexual or emotional abuse.

Bullying can become a serious problem. It can turn something as simple as recess or going to the bus stop into a nightmare for some kids. It can lead to serious emotional problems that scar a person for their entire life. In extreme cases it can lead to violence such as threats, property damage or someone getting seriously hurt as in suicide and suicide attempts.

That is why it is so important that you stand up against bullying. If you feel you are being bullied, take action to stop it.

the checklist

Entering the world of work often brings its own degree of uncomfortable attention. And as a woman, you should be up-front in dealing with it. For starters, you can make it clear to the offender that you are uncomfortable with his behavior. If it persists, you should report it to human resources and/or a superior. If the behavior goes unchecked, filing a formal complaint with the U.S. Equal Employment Opportunity Commission (EEOC) may be your only option.

chapter 6

Sorry ... I'm Too Stressed to Be Blessed

Hi, I'm a 9-1-1—an emergency
about to happen.

Happiness. To be happy.

When parents are asked what they want for their children's future, many of them answer with one of these two replies—"happiness" or "to be happy." Isn't that what you want for your children or for anyone you love?

Of course, values like "responsibility" show up on surveys specifically designed to measure values. But I bet if you asked 100 parents this question, "What do you wish for your child?" the answer would be "happy" more often than not, right?

But the focus of this book is not to talk to you about your children's happiness, although what I will talk about can greatly influence the happiness of your children and others in your life. What I want to talk about is YOU. Specifically, let's talk about how to have less stress and more joy in your own life.

You might be wondering, "Why is this important to me?"

Because when you have less stress and more joy in your life, it increases the likelihood that your children will grow up to be happy and they and other significant people in your life will benefit from your joy. Your joy, and the happiness of your child and those around you, will go a long way toward combatting a growing trend toward a highly stressful world.

You may be saying to yourself, "I don't get it?" And that's an appropriate response. So let's get started. You probably already know this intuitively, but I want to spell it out. A life filled with stress can impact your mental and emotional health and well-being.

And before we go further, let me clarify what I mean.

There are people who are born with mental health challenges such as personality disorders or schizophrenia. Those are not the mental health challenges I want to focus on in this book. Instead, in this chapter I want to focus on stress and mental health … how high stress levels rob you of joy. How stress can get in the way of healthy relationships, and how you can create less stress and more joy in your life.

Why? Let's face it; an environment where stress is not managed is an unhealthy environment for adults and children. Specifically, we are going to focus on three things:

1. What stress is and what it does to your health.

2. How you can manage your environment to manage your stress.

3. And thirdly, how you can manage your emotions to manage your stress.

You've probably been reading for a while now. So, let's start with an exercise. I'm going to ask you to write down three numbers. If you don't have a pen or pencil, then just try to remember your three numbers.

On a scale of 1-10, with one being low and ten being high, what is your level of stress during an average week?

- The number one means that you have no stress, which means you have no pulse!

- The number ten means that your family and friends have suggested you get some medication for your stress.

Next, on a scale of 1-10, with one being low and ten being high, what is your sense of humor during an average week?

- The number one means that you have no sense of humor.

- The number ten means that your family and friends have suggested you get some medication for that!

Finally, for your third number, on a scale of 1-10, how would you rate your ability to communicate effectively?

- The number one means that sometimes you either shut down or shut other people down.

- The number ten means that you communicate effectively with everyone you know!

Now, let's look at the results ...

Let's say that your stress level is high, your sense of humor is low, and you do not communicate effectively. So you might introduce yourself to someone like this:

"Hi, I'm a 9-1-1—an emergency about to happen."

So, what are your numbers?

You may be wondering why I introduced this exercise. Let's talk about it. When your stress goes up, what happens to your sense of humor? Yes, your sense of humor goes down. When your sense of humor goes down, what happens to your ability to communicate effectively? Yes, communication goes down. Now when you don't communicate well, what happens to your level of stress? Yes, it goes up. And as you can see, it all becomes a vicious cycle.

Let's stop the cycle by addressing stress today.

> Stress is anything that causes your energy level to go up.

One of the most confusing terms in the English language is stress. It is a verb. "I'm all stressed out." It is a noun; "I have too much stress in my life." So bottom line, "I am all stressed out because I have too much stress in my life!"

And what is stress really?

The bottom line is stress is anything that causes your energy level to go up. That is why things that are happy—weddings, social events, holidays—can also be very stressful. Simply because they require more energy.

Here's how it works. When your body senses that it needs an increase in energy, your body releases hormones such as cortisol and adrenaline to give you extra energy. This is like having your own personal Red Bull without the calories! This is actually good stress; it is called EUSTRESS.

Your body responds by giving you the energy boost you need to do whatever needs to be done, from automatically hitting the break when someone pulls out in front of you to doing a week's worth of house cleaning in 30 minutes, to chasing after a two year old just before the child reaches a flight of stairs.

Okay, after you have had a surge of adrenalin, how do you feel afterward? That's right, if you are anything like me, your energy level plummets. You have a sudden sinking feeling. That's because your body needs to rest.

In fact, in order for the cortisol and adrenaline to dissipate, your body needs to drop below your normal energy level. This space is called rest and relaxation. It is here that the body releases the built up hormones and returns to a healthy place.

But let's face it, for most of you, when you have a stressor in life, before you even get to your normal energy level something else happens ... and then something else ... and then something else. When that happens, you end up in distress, and that is when disease happens.

Let's take a minute and talk about some behaviors that people typically demonstrate when they are at this high level of stress. They are typically things like over-eating, drinking too much, depression, sleeping too much, not sleeping at all, and even violence and abusive behaviors.

In fact, there are people who live their entire adult lives in this realm. Perhaps you may even feel that you do. Sure, everyone has periods in life where stress is high. It is called acute stress. It is temporary and at some point you return to your "normal" energy level.

But, if you tend to live at this high level of stress, you have what is known as chronic stress. Your health—both physical and mental—will be compromised. There is much to be shared about the high cost of chronic stress. For now, I want you to understand what it is. And more importantly the impact it can have on your mental health and the mental health of your children and those around you.

Moods are contagious, aren't they? Think about it. As much as we hate to admit it, your children often reflect your mood, whether it is a positive one or a negative one. In fact, John Medina, author of *Brain Rules: 12 Principles for Surviving and Thriving at Work, Home, and School,* echoes this sentiment:

> The emotional stability of the home is the single greatest predictor of academic success. If you want your kid to get into Harvard, go home and love your spouse.

Let me paraphrase that a bit: The emotional health and mental health of your children are dependent on how parents manage their stress. If you want your kids to be happy and healthy, then learn to manage your stress.

So, now that you know a little about stress, let's look at three ways to manage stress in your world.

First, let's look at managing your environment. Your environment is composed of the following:

Your physical surroundings.

The information you allow into your brain.

The people that are in your life.

The question you have to ask yourself is whether or not these factors add to your sense of well-being or do they add stress to your life?

Let me repeat that.

Do these factors—your surroundings, the information or stuff you expose yourself to on a daily basis, the people in your life—add to your sense of well-being or do they add stress to your life?

Your Environment

Take a brief look at your environment. Is your physical

> Maintaining a sense of order can provide you with a stronger sense of control of your world.

world one that promotes calm or does it promote chaos?

Below are some statistics that might surprise you:

- It is estimated that the average American wastes 55 minutes a day looking for stuff. That's 12 days a year!

- In fact, when it's all added up, the average American spends one year of his or her life looking for lost or misplaced items.

- On the average, each morning you spend six minutes looking for your keys, or cell phone, or other routine items.

Maintaining a sense of order can provide you with a stronger sense of control of your world, but don't go overboard. That's called obsessive/compulsive disorder (OCD) and that can be a mental illness! So, remember, adults and children thrive in an organized environment, one that is calm and nurturing.

Next, what are you letting into your brain? What kinds of information do you bring into your world, specifically into your mind?

- Do you watch television programs that are anxiety-provoking or even violent?

- Is the news you watch an angry version of reality?

- Do you find yourself getting into word battles on Facebook or through text messages or emails?

- And speaking of Facebook, do you use it to connect with people in a meaningful way? Some research is suggesting that Facebook can often be depressing for people who compare their own lives with the lives of others.

My suggestion to you is that you make a point to surround yourself—and your children—with the kinds of information that stimulate curiosity, provokes thought, and evokes gratitude. When you do that, you will have less stress and more joy.

That brings us to the third component of your environment: People that are in your life.

Be conscious of the people you bring into your world, or you let stay in your world if they are already there. Truth be told, relationships can be healthy or they can be toxic. The people in your world can help you grow or they can hold you back. They can add to your self-esteem or they can diminish your self-esteem. They can help create a joyful environment or they can promote a stressful world.

I think you know the impact of toxic people in your life and the lives of your children.

So, let's focus for just a minute on people who have a positive influence on your mental health. An interesting characteristic of the people who promote a positive influence is that they seem to extend the perfect balance of being kind and being candid. This means that they demonstrate compassion and caring with encouraging words, seeing your potential and assuming the best. And, they are also candid.

- They can be honest without being mean-spirited.

- They can debate without being debilitating.

- They can be right without being righteous.

- And they can disagree without being disagreeable.

Having been in the mental health field for more than 25 years, I can promise you this. The environment in which you live and the people you surround yourself with have the capability to help you stress less and live more abundantly.

Manage Your Emotional Health

But there is another key to managing stress and achieving optimal mental health and that is to manage your emotional health. The three steps to managing your emotions are these:

1. Take control of your self-talk.

2. Be more positive.

3. Move forward.

Let's take a look at self-talk.

Do you ever have little voices in your head? You know the voice I'm talking about. It's kind of like a little invisible person standing on your shoulder shouting things in your ear, things like:

"If you were a good mother, or daughter, or employee, or volunteer, or a good anything, you would …."

Or, "Don't say anything; people will think you are stupid."

Or, "Be careful; don't make a fool of yourself!"

I call these voices the gremlins. Gremlins live inside your head or sit on your shoulder shouting negative messages to you. Surprisingly enough, they may sound like your mother, teachers, or other people in your life whose job it was to keep you from making mistakes. The only problem is that as you grew up, your voice forgot to take notice. It thinks of you as a child who needs help making the right decisions.

Another name for this voice is your roommate.

Now, please note that I am not talking about people with schizophrenic disorders who actually do hear voices in their head. I'm talking about the self-talk that holds you back instead of helping you move forward. Not only does this hold you back, this voice causes you a high level of stress because you doubt your own capabilities.

So here's the solution I recommend. Have a good conversation with your roommate. Ask yourself these questions and answer them with confidence.

When you hear a negative voice such as, "You will never get out of debt," or you end up ascribing a negative name to yourself such as, "You are such a loser," stop and ask yourself this question:

"Is it true?"

And then ask again, "Is it really true?"

And then again, "Is it really true all the time?"

Studies also show that when you use your name, you tend to listen more acutely to your inner talk.

Here's an example:

As I was working on the manuscript for this book, my roommate would pop up and say things like, "You are going to mess up!" "People are going to wonder if you know what you're talking about."

So I asked myself, "Danita, is that true?" — "No, Danita, it is not true."

"Danita, is that really true?" — "No, Danita, it is not really true."

"Danita, is that really, really true?" — "Of course not, Danita, it's not true at all."

Although if someone catches me having this conversation aloud with myself,

> Your self-esteem determines if you will take charge of your life.

they will indeed think I might be heading to an inpatient facility!

But you get the message, don't you? It's simple. You have to take control of the way you talk to yourself before you can take control of your life.

According to neuroscience, in order for you to have positive emotional health, you must give yourself three positive messages for every one negative message. If you give yourself one negative and one positive, you will have a negative image of yourself. If you give yourself one negative and two positives, your self-esteem is still compromised.

It is only when you give yourself three positive messages to every negative message that you can maintain a strong sense of self.

People ask me sometimes, "Is it possible to be overly positive in your self-talk?" And surprisingly, the answer is yes. In fact, research indicates that if you give yourself eleven or more positive messages to every one negative message, chances are you are living in "la la land," and that's not good mental health!

Here's another note for those of you who are parents or who work with children. Children need five positive messages to every one negative message to develop healthy self-esteem. That's right, a five to one ratio.

Here's what's important for you to remember. Your self-talk impacts your self-esteem. Your self-esteem determines if you will take charge of your life. And, if you want to manage the stress in your life, you are the one who must be in charge—not the people in your life or your gremlins.

There are many ways to add positivity in your life, such things as practicing gratitude or exercising on a regular basis. But one I particularly want to share with you is to spend money. Let me repeat that. Spend money. But don't spend money on stuff; rather spend it on experiences.

Let me assure you that eBay, Amazon, and local flea markets and yard sales are full of stuff that people spent money on, thinking the purchases would make them happy. Instead, spend your money on experiences for yourself like a "guilt free" dinner out, or a weekend getaway. When you do that, you not only have something to look forward to—another boost to positivity—but you have something special to remember.

This is another parenting suggestion; spend your money on giving your children experiences and not on giving them stuff. They will long remember the experience after the t-shirt is too small or thrown into the back of the closet.

Manage Interruptions and Your Time/ a Difficult Task

Time gets lost. People kill time. Time flies. It gets wasted. Time weighs heavy on your hands. You spend time. Time passes. It drags on or it hurries by. Those behind bars are said to be "doing time." Sometimes you have no time left; you're out of time.

According to the great American inventor Thomas Edison, "Time is really the only capital any human being has, and the one thing he can't afford to waste."

The perception of not having enough time for the things we must do or, just as importantly, the things we want to do is a leading cause of stress in society today. Continued exposure to stress can have an adverse effect on a person's health, both physical and mental.

Because you spend a great deal of your time at work, meeting your employer's expectations becomes increasingly important. Managing your time effectively, however, is often hampered by interruptions at work. Constant interruptions can significantly hinder effort, curtail creativity, and decrease productivity by disrupting thought processes and workflows, causing individuals to lose focus and take longer to complete tasks. A high rate of interruptions can be a serious issue in the workplace and can be a barrier to success.

Think back to your most recent day at work. I bet it went something like this. You arrive at work, sit down, and slowly begin to get into a groove. You begin working on that report that's due at the end of the day. After about an hour and a half, you quit to go to a meeting that was scheduled a few days ago. After the meeting you think, "What a waste of time. They could have just sent a memo for us to read and not interrupted my workday."

You go back to your office and try to get back to that report. The phone rings. It's Tom. You decide not to answer. Whatever it is, it can wait.

Two minutes later, Tom is knocking on your door. You bite your tongue and invite him in as you're thinking, "Can't he take a hint? I'm busy!" He spends twenty minutes discussing the meeting you just had and how he thought it was such a waste of time. He leaves.

The phone rings again. It's Jenny. You don't answer. You really need to get this report completed by the end of the day. Jenny sends you an email. You open it. She needs to discuss a matter of mutual concern regarding another work matter. She'd like to do this at your earliest convenience. You email her back that you will meet with her later in the afternoon. Gee, another meeting!

While emailing her, you notice several emails received since yesterday. You think, "Maybe I'll read some of these and get them out of the way." Two hours later, it's past lunch time and you haven't eaten. You take a break for lunch. When you return, Jenny is waiting to start the meeting you agreed to this morning.

Jenny leaves. Before you restart your computer, you decide to take a bathroom break. You run into John in the hallway. He comments that he hasn't seen you all day and wants to know what you've been up to. You tell him you have a report due and need to get back to it. The two of you talk for ten minutes.

You finish the conversation and complete that trip to the bathroom, resolving to get back to that report as soon as you get to your office. In your office, you remember a file you need to finish the report. You don't remember where you put it. After 30 minutes you locate it. Finally, you get back to your computer.

As you're typing away on your computer, your boss walks in, pats you on the shoulder and wants to know how it's going. You try to keep a straight face as you're thinking, "It could be going better if I could have avoided so many interruptions." After a brief conversation, you're alone again.

Controlling Interruptions

Does this sound familiar? If so, you may be experiencing "time stress." Learning to manage your time more effectively by controlling interruptions is the key to reducing stress and being more productive and successful on your job.

Here are some helpful strategies for taking control of your time and using it more effectively:

- Regularly organize and prioritize your work.

- Assess the types of interruptions you experience most. Are they necessary or not?

- Distinguish between available time and time that is off limits.

- Postpone unnecessary interruptions until you have some available time.

- Be willing to say "no." There are only so many hours in a day and only so much you can do with that time.

- Recognize that some interruptions are unavoidable. When these occur, encourage the interrupter to get to the point quickly. Don't engage in "small talk." Establish how much time you have to spare in the beginning, e.g., ten minutes, and stick to it.

Time management is a journey. By keeping control of your time and managing how it is spent, you may find that you have just a little more to spend.

Practice a Signature Strength

Another way to enhance positivity as a stress management technique is to practice a signature strength.

What are signature strengths you might be asking yourself? Signature strengths are the unique gifts that we each have been given. They can be things like:

- Hospitality
- Teaching
- Listening
- Problem solving
- Encouraging others
- Compassion
- Empathy
- Entertaining
- Humor
- And of course, parenting.

The list goes on and on. But here's what I know for sure, as Oprah would say, practicing a signature strength minimizes stress, enhances self-esteem and brings a positive feeling into your life.

So, I'm going to share two of my signature strengths with you.

One of my signature strengths is managing people and another is writing.

My life is more positive when I get to use my signature strengths. My sense of self is enhanced, and my stress is minimized.

What about you? Think about it. What are your signature strengths?

Sometimes when I work with women, someone will say, "But Danita, I have no signature strengths."

My response is always, "Of course you do." Just pay attention. You usually feel your best when you are using it. You are energized instead of stressed when using your signature strength. And other people usually benefit from the experience.

Move Forward

And now I'll share another skill in managing your emotions. It sounds so simple, yet can have a profound impact on your sense of self, your level of stress and your experience of joy.

It is to move forward. And by moving forward, I mean **don't get stuck in a rut.**

> **1. Let go of past failures and pains.** Regret, guilt and fixation on the bad things that happened in your past can prevent you from moving forward in the present and into the future. You can no longer control the past, but you can prevent the past from controlling you.
>
> **2. Don't surrender control to other people.** Your life is yours to live. Don't let people put you in a box because of such things as race, gender or age.

Others may offer guidance and advice. Some of this can be helpful, and some of it can be hurtful. Regardless, you need to make decisions based on your own desires and ideas without worrying about what others expect of you.

3. **Quit running away.** Problems and issues inevitably arise, and many of these issues cannot be avoided forever. The more time you waste on running away, the less time you have for moving forward. For instance, if there is a misunderstanding or other form of tension between you and someone else, try talking it out with that person. The relationship could break apart afterward, but it could also end up becoming stronger. Either way, the issue will only continue to fester in your life until you take care of it.

4. **Drop the excuses.** Granted, there are often legitimate obstacles that may prevent you from pursuing a specific goal or idea, but oftentimes, something one considers to be an obstacle can be overcome with a little effort. When there is an obstacle that you can remedy, telling yourself that it prevents you from accomplishing something is simply an excuse, and these excuses need to stop.

One of the primary reasons so many women live in a chronic state of stress is that they don't take the time to enjoy life. They are always too busy putting out fires. It's always about their kids, their spouses, their jobs, even their elderly parents.

the checklist

Stop, yes, stop and take time for you. Step back and consider your own needs. You need to learn to stop, take a break, sit down and put your feet up. Apologies for taking time for you are not necessary. After all, the less stress in your life will have a residual effect on everyone else in your life.

chapter 7

Making a Case for Personal Change

Either planned or unplanned,
the challenges presented by change can disrupt your life
in such a way that it causes emotional distress.

When it comes to change, noted author Max DePree (*Leadership is an Art*) is credited with saying *"We cannot become what we need to be by remaining what we are."*

Most people want to change something about themselves. But as most of you already know, change is hard!

I have found that the best way to start on a path to change is to start with changing your mindset. The desire and ability to change your mind, the way you think, can have a positive effect on changing your life.

Your mind is very powerful. The only person that can cause you to make a change is you. It starts with you and your attitude toward change. If you believe that there is nothing you can do to effect change in your life, you are probably right. But, if you believe that change is possible, then you are also right. The question is what do you believe?

Whether change in your life is planned or unplanned, it is often challenging. A planned change might be your deciding to re-enroll at the local university to complete that degree that you started several years ago and never finished. Or it might be the New Year's resolution you made to lose twenty pounds.

Unplanned change can be as simple as your child missing the school bus causing you to have to drive her to school and be late for work and suffering the wrath of your boss. Or, it can be more catastrophic like your employer announcing that the company has decided to downsize and gives you a pink slip at the end of the workday.

Either planned or unplanned, the challenges presented by change can disrupt your life in such a way that it causes emotional distress. If serious enough, it can even feel as if you are stuck on a runaway train and you have no ability to stop it from plummeting down the hill in front of you.

But personal change can be managed.

Melba's Story

"I was 21, I was a teacher, and I hated it," says Melba Moore to me on a warm morning in late July. We're sitting in a borrowed boardroom in midtown Manhattan, 24th floor, for the interview, and she's filling that imposing space with her energy, her fire, and her humor.

> I was good at it, she continues. It was the job that
> everyone expected me to take. It was one decent
> job I could get as a young black woman in the
> '60s. My parents were pleased. And you know
> what? I was miserable.

We're talking about turning points in life—and failure and change. These are subjects I know well.

Listening to Melba, my mind goes back to when I was seven, standing in the living room of our shabby house in Gary, Indiana. My younger sister and older brothers were with me. The four of us were lined up in front of our father, and he was furious with me.

"You are so stupid!" he said. We were having a family meeting. My mother had left with my baby sister the day before, fed up with my father's abuse.

Before the meeting, my father assured us that we could and indeed should speak our minds. He told us that he wanted the "straight truth" from each of us. We nodded our heads warily. He went on to tell us that he and my mother might be getting a divorce. He asked each of us in turn who we wanted to live with should this come to pass, my mother or him.

My older brothers and sister had experienced enough of my father's temper to have learned a thing or two. All three of them answered that they would like to live with both mother and him. Those were the words my father wanted to hear.

Then he turned to me. "Who do you want to live with, little girl?" I didn't even hesitate. If it was the truth he wanted, then I would give it to him. "I want to live with my mother," I said as firmly as a seven year old can. And that's when all the shouting began.

"You are so stupid!" my father shouted. "You'll never amount to anything. You're worthless. I don't know why I have to feed you. What use are you?" I tried to make myself as small as I could. I didn't understand. He wanted the truth, didn't he?

At 21, Melba tells me, she was wrestling with the same demon.

> A young woman just by nature has to be confused. You've been trained to listen and take orders from your parents, your elders, but not trained to listen to what's going on with yourself.

So she was miserable, because she was doing what everyone else wanted her to do, but not what her heart knew she needed to do.

> Fortunately, the heart is always powerful! You have to listen to those that have been here before you. But you have to take it in, and mix it with who you're learning to be. You need to be aware of the heart inside you.

I ask her how she discovered her talent to sing.

> My parents were show people—they wanted me to get a real job. My mother was a singer, and a single parent. I was raised by a nanny, who also cared for my invalid grandmother. I grew up with anger, abuse, and a broken family around me

until I was nine. Then my mother remarried into
a nice middle-class family. It was culture shock!

I did learn to adjust. Whatever difficulties I had,
they were well worth it. It's a good problem to try
to adjust to a happy, healthy life. But I was still
angry underneath. I saw my parents performing,
living, talking and dreaming the music business,
and I caught that bug.

"How do you tell the difference between a real talent,
and just wanting to be a celebrity?" was one of my questions
for her:

Observe yourself. What keeps coming into your
heart and your mind?

I'm responding to Melba internally; my head is spinning.

*But it's hard to be certain when there's pain and confusion
all around you. It took me many years before I realized that
I had been raised in a house full of chaos. My father was a
very angry man. He was comfortable as a victim, blaming
everyone else for all his problems and lack of success. It was
an excuse for not trying and for not making better choices.
It affected everyone and everything around him.*

*For us kids, it meant hard times. We wore hand-me-down
clothes. We put cardboard in our shoes to cover the holes in
the soles. We had no indoor toilet.*

*Failure was the very air we breathed. It was what was
expected of us. As a matter of fact, if we had our little victories
in life like a good report card or a kind word from someone
on the block, we were ridiculed by my dad. "You think you're*

smarter than everyone else?" He would say. "You think you're better than everyone else, don't you?" That was my dad. When we wanted kindness, we got sarcasm. When we needed guidance, we got indifference. I don't think he was aware of how his words affected us.

I have wondered many times why I didn't just pack it in? Failure is the easy option, after all. And not just for a young girl. It is easy for us all. I saw our poverty as a failure. It was a failure to have a father like mine.

But in the end there's a kind of comfort in it. Failure tells us that all we have to do is give up and it will all be over.

Melba told me how she kept from giving up, with everyone telling her to be happy she was a teacher, yet knowing inside she wanted to sing.

> I had to retrace my steps, she says. I was depressed. I was pugilistic—fighting all the time. I was angry. You have to take one little thing at a time. Write it down, just one idea; say to yourself, "I'm just going to look at that." You have to replace the negative with something positive. What are some of the possibilities you have that might replace that "can't"? That's how you make yourself a little bit stronger where you were weak. For me, I wanted to get rid of my pugilistic tendencies, because if you are angry the first person you hurt is you. I learned that. Then I learned to go back and retrace why it happened. How can I do it differently? How can I make the choice not to be angry? I wanted to sing, and I believed in God. I think those are the two positive things that saved me.

Watching Melba speak, watching her fill the room with her energy, I think that there's one other thing that's important too. And that's a sense of self. You have to believe that you matter.

Failure is always there ready, talking to us, sometimes in a whisper and sometimes through a bullhorn.

The challenge is to resist the pull. Failure will inevitably come and a strong sense of yourself is essential to fighting back.

I'm lucky, like Melba Moore, because even though I came from a failure-rich background, from my earliest memory I have had the blessing of a strong sense of self. I wanted to count. I wanted to amount to something. I knew I wasn't stupid. I was determined to prove my father wrong.

Did my father's words hurt me that afternoon? Yes! Even today, if I am having a particularly bad day, I can still feel their sting. I wanted so badly to please my daddy! It was tough for me to feel that I had failed him.

And yet somehow I knew—just knew—that I had it in me to be intelligent and talented and giving. I'd had other people, people close to me tell me so—my mother, grandmother, my first grade teacher Mrs. Kaufman, and my oldest sister. And I believed them. Why wouldn't I? They knew a lot more about life than I did and if they said I was an amazing, wonderful kid, who was I to disagree? They taught me to never ever apologize for my natural gifts.

That's what you've got to learn to do with failure. You've got to NOT let it define you. Let success define you. Use the failure to see how you can do better and how you can make a positive change.

Don't blame someone else if it is your failure, but don't let it become part of you. Use it for the lessons it teaches you, and move on. Move on to success.

Melba shared how she moved on, in those first hard days.

> I talked to my parents, she remembers. They were shocked. But in the end, since they were show business people, they had to understand. They supported me. They introduced me to some people, and I started singing jingles. Its good work, the pay is decent, and you get the residuals if the ad is played over and over.

"But how did you get from working behind the scenes to becoming a household name?" I want to know.

Melba smiles,

> One of the recording sessions I was in turned out to involve the people who were producing **Hair**. I had never heard of it. I don't have a BA in music to do nobody's hair. Sometimes you are in situations when you can't plan; sometimes you need faith. I wound up in **Hair** and stayed in it for 18 months. I auditioned for the lead and got it. Then, one of the girls in the chorus told me about auditions for another Broadway show that was starting up. I auditioned for the lead of **Purlie**, with Phil Rose, the director. I got the part, the show got a Tony award, and that's what put me on the map.

It's clear to me that Melba has something else that we all need to overcome the failures—courage to keep trying. You'll get scars along the way, like Melba did. I've gotten my share too.

But scars are beauty marks, not wounds. We should wear them as badges of honor and not marks of shame. There is a story in each one.

> The best thing about scars, says Melba, is that in the long run they give you a nice thick skin! The benefits of thick skin are truly magnificent. After a while, the little stuff begins to bounce off of you. And I can tell you that's really important in the music business.

Melba continues, "Misery dis-empowers you. You have to protect yourself. You have to keep working. You have to have focus."

By the time I was in high school, I had my thick skin and my strong sense of self. I felt powerful! And unfortunately for me, I thought that was all I would ever need. Soon, I fell in with the wrong crowd. It was round-the-clock party time. I was the cut-up, the sarcastic one. We had fun and not much else.

It drove my father around the bend, which for me was an added bonus. If he didn't like it, then I knew I surely did. Soon though, the joke was on me. I was pregnant, kicked out of school, and I gradually realized that my friendships only lasted as long as the good times did. Yes, I had a first-rate sense of self and I was the proud owner of a leathery hide, but I was missing the third key ingredient that I needed to add to the mix: I hadn't learned from failure to keep trying to succeed.

The social group I had chosen for myself at sixteen, as fun as it was at times, was an empty husk. Nobody spoke of aspirations. Talk of dreams and goals was non-existent. Whatever any of the other members of the group wanted to do, well, that was fine with the rest of us. You want to stay out past curfew and miss school? Great! Go for it! Absolutely!

It was to say the least, anything goes. And everything went. The biggest problem was that no one challenged anyone else in the group. I soon stopped challenging myself. I drifted from moment to moment, from party to party, all the while digging the hole a little deeper every day. Without realizing it or intending to do so, I had recreated my home life all over again. Just like before, failure was everywhere I looked.

Thankfully, at that point, I understood that I had to make a change. I had a baby daughter of my own and other bills to pay. Finally, I had had enough! I began to look for work but without even a high school diploma, I had little luck.

I remember reading the descriptions of jobs in the want ads and I would say to myself, "I know I can do that job!" I met the people who did those jobs and they weren't any more capable than I was. They did, however, have the diploma that I did not possess. All of the passion and purpose in the world wouldn't get me a decent job if it required a diploma.

Melba, who was at the top of show business with a Tony and all the success she could handle, found herself a manager and boyfriend in one, and then lost it all. She got pregnant, and he persuaded her to get an abortion. There were complications, and it took a year to recover. In that year, her boyfriend left and took all her money. She found herself back at home, taking care of her mother who was dying. She had lost all that she had gained except one thing: she still had her talent. She began the long, slow climb back.

I had my own climb to do. I finally went back and passed my high school equivalency exam. For me, and for Melba, on different journeys, it was the same message: one slow day at a time.

I remember the advice of some of my elders growing up. The message was "You can do anything you put your mind to." That is indeed a wonderful message. It's nice to hear, but you need to act on it. That's what you can learn from failure: to keep trying.

If you set forth only two options for yourself, everything or failure, you are headed for a train wreck. Ask any gambler. They will tell you that winning or losing are all that exist. It is like trying to get your bearings by looking in all directions at once. It gets quite disorienting.

Instead, set a small goal you know you can meet and then achieve that goal. Goals should feel real, ordinary, everyday. Goals should be something you can look in the face and not be overwhelmed. Failure loves you to set unattainable goals for they are rarely met.

I think of the millions of people all over the world who have had their lives saved in twelve-step programs. I have had the privilege of watching their courage and dedication from close range. I have sat across the desk from people I never thought could break a drug habit or quit drinking do just that.

Somehow they were able to draw on a deep, invisible reservoir of resolve that allowed them to break the downward negative spiral that was ruining their lives. They were able to come back from failure and reach a goal of sobriety. They did so by setting small goals, one day at a time.

I have also witnessed individuals that I thought had all the right stuff to break a substance habit, fail and re-enter their addiction. Invariably, the ones that succeeded chose to see their struggle as a new and winnable battle that they fought every day. Those who failed tended to look at the fight as "Me against all my demons." This latter mindset is a well-trodden path to failure.

The twelve-step rule of "One day at a time" was arrived at through much painful trial and error. Its wisdom is subtle and powerful. The road to healing is laid one paving stone at a time. I think it is important to remember what you can learn from their struggle and triumph—*one slow day at a time*. In our all or nothing culture, when we miss the glory of getting it all the failure of nothing is the only consolation prize.

For me, passing that high school equivalency exam was the goal that I met, but my struggle was far from over. But, I managed to finally land a job. Times were tough for job hunting. Through some people I knew, I was able to finally land employment. Was it my dream job? Hardly. I was on the bedpan brigade at the local mental hospital. I was furious! This was the best I could do? I thought myself much better than the work I was doing. Fairly quickly, my resentment began to bubble to the surface. I started to show up late for work. My attitude gradually eroded. I was quick to snap at my fellow employees.

One particular evening, I was late for the umpteenth time and my supervisor pulled me aside. She told me I was late more often than not. She pointed out that my attitude was unpleasant, to put it mildly. I was one step from a pink slip, she said. I told her that I was angry. She replied quietly, maybe even a little sadly, "You're always angry."

She was right. Nothing was good enough for me. I always expected better. And that was setting me up for another failure.

I felt that I was entitled to a better life. I spent untold amounts of mental and even physical energy feeding the anger inside me. It was familiar and it made me feel good, but only for a little while. My anger often left me isolated and empty, and it always wanted to be fed with more conflict.

Slowly I saw that the anger inside me was crowding out everything else. There was no room inside me for love or even a sense of humor. And stoking that anger all the time was tiring. I saw that I had to put that burden down and when I did, I found that I had unexpected focus and energy in reserve.

I transferred all that negative energy into achieving my goals instead. And I needed every bit of that new-found energy to get to where I am now. I often had to work twice as hard as other people to achieve my goals. I was able to get my four-year degree and then my master's. Step by step, I struggled forward to each finish line that I had set for myself.

Today, Melba Moore has a new album, a new career, and a great support team helping her to achieve her goals.

> Think about what you have that is valuable to others, she says. How can you help them? What do they want out of this situation? Get out of your own needs and desires. See if you can figure out what their dreams are. If you can help someone

else along the road to their dreams, they will help you in return.

Success is an intricate process, but it begins simply by trying again in the face of failure. Failure is the starting point for success. If you keep trying, setting small, every-day goals for yourself, success will come.

> Change can be good and you can learn to embrace it, rather than run from it.

Success or failure: the choice is yours. You own it. It's a choice you must and can make alone. Remember though, you are more than enough.

Melba shares,

We can learn skills, but what we really need to learn is virtue. Virtue keeps trying. That's what makes a person valuable. In that virtue, you'll one day find joy. Joy rejuvenates you, makes you smarter and really pisses your enemies off!

Change is about personal growth.

As you can see, change is difficult. At least that's what most people believe, so they avoid it, though it doesn't have to be that way. Change can be good and you can learn to embrace it, rather than run from it. It just takes a shift in your perspective.

The world today is complex. Advances in technology means everyone is working faster, harder and longer than ever before. Priorities are misaligned as we attempt to be it all and do it all. When a change in our personal or profes-sional life occurs, our lives become even more complicated.

The change might be small, like going to a 10 o'clock doctor's appointment and having to wait longer than expected. The change might be large, like the unexpected loss of a close friend. Either way, change is like being at the epicenter of an earthquake; your world is rocked. Sometimes it's just a jolt of movement that snags your attention. Other times, precious valuables are knocked off your shelves as you attempt to regain your footing after a massive change.

Yes, change is difficult. Yet, there are steps you can take to make change—big or small—more manageable:

- **The only person you can change is you.** It is natural to want to push people to change, particularly those we love. But it is a known fact that most people do not change until they are psychologically and emotionally ready to. The Serenity Prayer adopted by Alcoholics Anonymous many years ago goes like this:

  God grant me the serenity to accept the things I cannot change, the courage to change the things I can, and the wisdom to know the difference. —Reinhold Niebuhr

  In this prayer, it is apparent that there are many things you cannot change because you have no control over them, but there are some things you can change beginning with you. The best way to help other people change is to change your own behavior. The changes that others see in you can inspire them to want to change. Your change experience can even help you to learn a little about human behavior that you can impart to others in their desire to make a change.

- **Know yourself.** The 24/7 nature of today's world can make it hard to slow down and tune in to your natural tendencies and rhythms. With a strong sense of self, you are better equipped to manage change. When change occurs, how does it affect you? Do you worry? Do you become anxious? Do you get excited about new opportunities? You might jot down your thoughts to uncover a pattern you never noticed before.

- **Assess your attitude.** Your attitude is everything. How you perceive change affects the outcome of that change. For example, if you receive news that your employer is struggling to keep the doors open. To help save jobs, the CEO has decided to cut salaries by 10 percent. You just bought a new car. How do you respond? What is your attitude? Do you resist the change or look at it as an opportunity to do something different?

- **Build a support network.** "Lean on me, when you're not strong; And I'll be your friend; I'll help you carry on." Bill Withers knew what he was talking about in his popular song "Lean on Me." Everyone needs support. The most successful people in the world would not have achieved their level of success without a strong network of supportive people. You're no different. In any stage of life, but especially during change, seek and embrace the help of family, friends, peers, and mentors.

- **Reset your goals.** Change is hard because it requires you to reset your plans. Often you become so attached to your vision that it's difficult to let it go. Even worse, you become attached to the how of reaching your vision. You've made plans. You've decided the path. You don't want anything to get in the way. Then change does just that; it gets in the way. When change occurs, stop, get your bearings and reassess your goals. You may continue to pursue the same goals or you may choose an alternate path. In either case, use change as an opportunity to reevaluate what you want.

- **Believe in yourself.** You can accomplish great things. Change is an inevitable part of life. It happens and it will continue to happen over and over again. While there will be periods of uncertainty when change occurs, you must believe that you can navigate it successfully and that you'll come out of it a better person.

the checklist

People who master change understand that change happens in life. They also view change as a learning experience. Change is an opportunity to understand yourself better, redefine your perspective, connect with others and reevaluate your future. Change is about personal growth. When you embrace change and learn from it, you will uncover opportunities to profit from it and use it as a tool to teach others. Change is good.

chapter 8

The Challenges of Leadership

Being a woman is a terribly difficult task,
since it consists principally in dealing with men.
—Joseph Conrad, author

Male vs Female Leadership Effectiveness

Gentlemen, if you are reading this, you might want to skip past this section.

Ladies, this is primarily for you. Because I want to share a little secret with you, a secret that probably isn't a secret to you at all: Women really ought to be in charge.

Don't get me wrong. Some of my best friends are men, and I'm married to a wonderful one. But the sad fact is that the overwhelmingly male dominated leadership in this country at all levels—societal, governmental, even in business—has not withstood the test of time. As we look at world events, crime statistics, the economy, our educational system, even health care, we know that there is still so much work to be done.

It truly should be the women's turn to step up and try leadership roles for a while. You could hardly do any worse. I'll give you an example: Nine out of ten men who have read this so far have probably dismissed my assertions out of hand. A good percentage of women probably did as well, at first. But then, I'm betting the vast majority of these women returned to the idea and gave it some good, hard thought. It is that capacity for thoughtfulness, I maintain, about even highly volatile emotional issues that makes women the better choice to be in leadership roles.

Recently I was reviewing some of the material I've had an opportunity to study as a means of staying on top of new thinking in the areas of leadership and management, issues of vital importance to me in my day-to-day existence, and to all of you in your overall lives. Two sources of information in the realm of leadership and business management struck me as right on target in regard to the need for women to assume greater responsibility than we now have. Taken together, the two sources provide compelling arguments.

First there is the book *Our Emperors Have No Clothes* by Alan Weiss, PhD. Dr. Weiss probably made few friends in the upper echelons of the business world by naming names and pulling no punches when it came to criticizing the white male-dominated management structure of corporate America.

Next, the website of the California-based Hagberg Consulting Group leadership training organization offers strong evidence that now, perhaps more than ever, is the time when women should move to the fore. But how can that happen if you are hiding out in the shadows?

The latter source delivers details of a workplace study in which employees surveyed rated women superior to men in such traditional management skills as hiring, coaching and developing subordinates, and organizing as well as monitoring the work of others. "Women's management style, which centers around communication and positive working relationships, is better suited than men's to the team-oriented leadership of (today)," according to Hagberg Consulting Group. Women, the organization's study showed, have better social skills, are better at communication, keep people informed, put the success of the team first and use influencing skills rather than authority.

By contrast, Dr. Weiss suggests in *Our Emperors Have No Clothes* that in the fat, dumb and happy years following World War II, even mediocre business people prospered and the organizations over which they had influence grew. Increasing levels of management, often with little or no connection to producing a product or service, also grew. Through a pernicious system of sponsorships, by which top managers bring along their successors, Weiss contends many poor management techniques and practices have been perpetuated. "The power structure in most organizations remains predominantly white male," Weiss writes.

> There is significant risk in sponsoring someone
> who is not like you, and a white woman, minority

male or, especially, a minority woman represents high "risk." What if one of these people chooses to dress differently, or deliberately uses nonstandard English, or demands a holiday that is not on the approved list? The bottom line to all of this is that stupid management, like an amoeba, has a method of recreating itself.

So, fellows, consider yourselves warned: Women might be able to "manage" just fine without you.

Women Leading the Way

What do you really know about leadership? Leading is not easy. Good leaders are rare and great ones are worth their weight in diamonds. The big question for you is can you, as a leader, take your ideas, your passions, and work with the contrary forces that life throws your way? Your success or failure as a leader relies on your ability to apply your best-laid plans in what the old Chinese saying calls "interesting times." And times are always interesting—never simple, never easy—don't you agree?

Leadership involves convincing people that change is necessary and yet change, even the best kind imaginable, brings with it a certain amount of pain. Thus the question for the leader is: can I get people to go with me and accept the pain, discomfort, and the "shock of the new" to get to a better place?

It's About Them

Without followers, there are no leaders. Many would-be leaders forget this. They become wrapped up in their great ideas and in the ways they will solve difficult problems by the sheer force of their will. That's not what leadership is.

The secret of a leader lies in her ability to get people to follow her on a challenging journey to a new, unknown place that is far outside of the usual comfort zone.

You can have the most fantastic, innovative ideas in the world and if you cannot succeed in getting the buy-in of those you are attempting to lead, then all of your efforts will ultimately fall short. Former Democratic candidate for President, Howard Dean, had a motto that he quoted many times on the campaign trail. The motto was: It's the people, stupid!" Dean was reinforcing what every leader should have burned into her mind. It's about the people you are attempting to lead. A leader by definition has people behind her. If she does not, she is not a leader. A leader spends huge amounts of time considering the landscapes of the minds and hearts of the people she is trying to lead.

Some considerations a leader should make about those they wish to lead:

Who are "they?" Are they senior, junior, or at my level? Are they young or have they been around the block? What do they like to do for fun? Are they stressed out or engaged and happy? What frightens them? What are their dreams and their fears? Spend some time getting to know the people you want to lead before you try to lead them.

How will they feel about a new way of doing things? Are they excited about a novel approach or are they afraid or even belligerent about the idea of change? What push-back are you likely to encounter? Have they "been there, done that?" What concerns and questions will they bring to the table? Have similar initiatives like yours failed in the past? Always remember that a leader has to know what the people have experienced in their past with your particular organization.

How will they feel about you? What is your track record as a leader? Are you trustworthy? Are you known or unknown to these people? Are you considered a good listener? Are you seen as thoughtful? Will they see you as a know-it-all or will they see you as an innovator? Will they believe that you are keeping their best interests at heart or will they tag you as self-interested? Ask yourself how you would feel if you were being led by you! When it is a question of how others see you, remember that for better or worse, perception is often reality.

You should spend some time seriously considering each of the above concepts. Also, it is imperative that you be brutally honest with yourself. Delusion is a deadly trait in a leader. If you are a bad listener, admit it and start being a good one. If you are unknown to these folks, don't assume they will love you because of your beautiful smile. When you truly consider the human side of those you lead, you are well on your way to being a real leader.

Remember that you may have strong opinions on how you want to lead, but the people you may want to lead have even stronger feelings about how they want to be led.

Think Strategically and Plan How to Implement Your Strategy

A good leader will work long and hard to come up with a plan. Great leaders also know that things don't always go as planned and so they create a fallback plan. Effective leaders don't enter the leadership arena saying, "Well, I'll just wing it." An award-winning actress or a celebrated operatic singer would never think of hitting the stage without having practiced every word of the script or every note of her song to perfection. Preparation is the key to your success and you can never over-prepare. Failing to consider all angles could be disastrous. A real leader has considered all the potential scenarios, and consequently she is rarely surprised.

Your plan should be a sure blueprint of your ideas. Your plan should include the input of others. Your plan should transform something that is "yours" into something that is "ours."

When you let people have input even over things you may see as trivial, you can create group ownership of your idea. Once you find out what people in your group are good at, get their feedback on the plan and then put them to work. Tasking each group member with those things where he or she has knowledge and skills guarantees that everyone has an opportunity to participate. Don't come across as a know-it-all. If you do, you will quickly find that you will have to be a do-it-all as well. Your inevitable burn out could likely derail the project.

Your plan should also have one irrefutable characteristic. It should be malleable. We've all heard about the folly of the best-laid plans of mice and men. The same goes for the plans of leaders. A great leader is always able to recognize when a plan isn't working the way it should or when a better plan comes along. When you remain open to change, you have the ability to see the entire realm of possibility. When you refuse to consider change, it's like going through life wearing a blindfold.

Be ready for change and embrace it warmly.

You Can't Go It Alone

In America we have a strange obsession with the idea of going it alone. The Clint Eastwood-type character taking off ahead of the pack, independent and fearlessly blazing the trail is the image that readily comes to mind. Going it alone is a romantic notion captured brilliantly by Sinatra who sang defiantly of doing it "my way." Our notions of leaders are much the same. The prevailing image of a leader is an individual who is willing to go it alone, risking all of the glory of being the lone voice of reason and truth. That leader then looks around from her illustrious throne only to find that it is lonely at the top. Nothing could be further from the truth.

It turns out that the best leaders are those who have a strong network of people whom they can call upon for help in making crucial decisions. Self-aware leaders know that wise decisions are not made in isolation. When making decisions, leaders often have a group of trusted advisors and they can call upon individuals in the group for advice and support. Some in the group may have been through the same trials and tribulations that you find yourself in. As a novice leader it is important to find those people who can help you, and when you discover them, hang on to them for dear life. You must depend on others sometimes to help you reach your goals.

There is an important distinction to be made between "yes" people and those who will tell you the cold, hard truth that you need to hear. Surrounding yourself with yes people is one of the most dangerous things you can do. Instead, try nipping this in the bud by hiring trustworthy people who are willing to disagree.

You don't want to surround yourself with all people who think like you. Too much of the same thing can inhibit growth. You want to have diversity and alternative points of view. A supportive person is not just someone who is a tireless advocate for you and your ideas. A supporter doesn't look at you through rose-colored glasses. Supporters are realists who nurture, affirm, and support you on a healthy journey of life but are willing to tell you the truth to keep you from making mistakes.

You might ask yourself, "Where do I find supporters?" Some of your most ardent supporters will likely be found in places that you might not normally think of. They might be people from industries or business environments that are very different from yours. These advisors can give you a perspective that you may not have ever thought about. A close friend, your pastor, or even your physician might all be able to provide you with some great insight. Seeking diversity and breadth of opinion may be one of your greatest assets as a successful leader.

Be aware that, as you move up in the leadership ranks, you will come in contact with those who are insincere and disingenuous in their support for you. One thing to be careful of on your hunt for supportive people is the trap of toxic supporters and naysayers. You don't want people who bring your mood down with their pessimism, anxiety, and general sense of distrust. They will pretend they are on your side and secretly do everything they can to undermine your success. They are usually not out to get you or to be cruel. They are typically unhappy because of their own failures in life. Because of their insecurities, and their need to not feel bad about themselves, they find it difficult to support your goals or respect the time and effort you put in to achieve them.

Having toxic people in your life can have a negative effect on your attitude and can compromise your ability to reach your goals. Toxic people can be excruciatingly difficult to deal with because of their negative attitudes and their ability to dampen your mood or enthusiasm.

Therefore, select your supporters carefully. If you do find toxic supporters, don't let them into your inner circle. Your inner circle should be a place of privilege, reserved only for the select few. Be polite. Be civil. But don't be stupid. Keep them at arm's length.

Believe in Yourself

It's been said that you are born alone and you die alone. Some people see that as a sad thing. To me, it's joyous, resounding proof that all of the power and wisdom needed in this life resides within each of you. Each of you has yourself and that, in some profound way, is more than enough.

I'm not suggesting that you were put on this earth to go it alone. On the contrary, other people are one of the most precious gifts that you are given as a leader and as a human being. People are a tremendous wellspring of love, support, and wise counsel. That being said, when I think back about the toughest decisions that I've been faced with, in the end, it all came down to me. You will find that it will often be the same for you.

Like it or not, every leader has to make the call when the occasion arises. Experience shows us that letting others make the big choices for us can be ill-advised to say the least. Of course, we've all been there. We've listened to the wrong advice and if we are lucky, we end up with a bad haircut. Unfortunately for those who desire to be leaders, the stakes are often much higher.

Certainly you may agree on important choices with a life partner or family member or friend. That is what they are there for. But when it all comes down to it, your conscience, your experience, and your expertise must be your ultimate guides. Collectively, they are the sextant that you use to chart your course in a complex world.

In the End, Leadership All Comes Down to You

A great leader trusts others as she trusts herself. She believes in her abilities and in the abilities of those in her support group. When the critical moment comes, she will be unafraid to act, knowing that she has considered all the angles and personalities. She can take comfort in the counsel she has sought and in the opinions she has taken into account. In the words of Harvard leadership expert Ron Heifitz, the great leader reaches the critical moment when she must "come down off the balcony."

If she has done the hard work of assessing the needs of those she desires to lead, if she has crafted a plan and a fallback plan, if she has sought out a positive group of supporters, and if she ultimately has an unshakable, unquenchable belief in herself, then she is well on her way to becoming a great leader. It is a long steep process with no shortcuts. If leadership was easy, there would only be leaders with no followers. But there is always room for a new generation of leaders.

Great leaders are not born; rather they are forged from the white-hot fires of life experience.

Leading Through Change

Many would-be leaders miss the deeper principle: to be a leader you must have influence over your followers.

It's easy to get someone to follow you. Roles and hierarchies within organizations make leadership transactional — "Joe, this is your boss Anita. Follow her." But it's up to you to make leadership relational. Your relationship with your followers is the sweet spot where true leadership happens.

> To turn Edgewater Systems around, I would have to make many changes.

This is especially true when leading through change. And when is a leader not managing some type of change?

Leading through change isn't easy. I know this from having led a number of troubled organizations in my career. Upon joining Edgewater Systems, I found the organization was in a state of complete chaos—on the brink of bankruptcy, revoked operating license, low employee morale—and about to close its doors.

I would have to make many changes to turn Edgewater Systems around. Some changes would be welcomed, while others would be met with heavy resistance. My biggest dilemma was how could I get people to accept the discomfort of change and follow me into an unknown future?

Here's what I discovered worked best:

Realize that it's not about you. At the most basic level of human interaction, people want to be seen, heard and understood. Many leaders overlook this and leap straight into goals and action plans. Slow down. Spend time getting to know your people. Think about who they are, where they fit in the organization, what they dream and hope for, what they fear, what contributions they want to make.

Create a sense of urgency. Most people don't enjoy the disruption of change. Your goal is to shift them from wanting things to be better to being willing to make things better. You do this by creating a sense of urgency and communicating why change must occur. Speak to their needs and desires. Show them the direct consequences of ignoring change—make it urgent.

The nature of change is that it continues to change! In any situation there are too many variables to predict, many of which are outside of your immediate control. Cast a vision for your people, put a plan in motion and navigate the hills and valleys of change along the way.

I've already stated that leading through change isn't easy. I've had varying degrees of success in my leadership career, and it hasn't been perfect. Even after many years of experience, I continue to learn and grow as a leader.

Sometimes leadership requires making hard decisions and choosing a path that goes against the norm. Leadership takes courage. It has been said that the lack of courage, in management and in life, is perhaps the most critical factor in determining whether you will succeed or fail as a leader. Organizations today need leaders who are unencumbered by fear. More courageous leaders are needed who can guide them through troubled times in spite of the challenges and help organizations serve up successful turnarounds.

> Your goal is to shift people from wanting things to be better to being willing to make things better.

In today's economic climate, there are masses of people seeking a turnaround. Lives have been ruined by financial circumstances that have created challenges that many struggle to overcome. Layoffs, downsizing, mortgage foreclosures, declining 401K plans, among others, have all contributed to a general malaise in the workplace and in the personal lives of many. Many leaders are afraid to add to the emotional burdens of a work force that is already seeing unprecedented hardship. They may even be experiencing many of the same difficulties themselves. As a result, the courage to pursue a turnaround, both organizationally and personally, is declining. Quite simply, many people are afraid of what the future might bring.

Unfortunately fear can be paralyzing. It can hold you back and keep you from realizing your optimum potential. The fears of change, of loss, of being wrong, or of being embarrassed, are examples of emotional barriers that can rob you of opportunities for happiness and success. These emotional barriers often get in the way of opportunities for positive change. Your ability to move through these barriers and to muster the courage to move beyond your fears is the hallmark of an effective leader.

> Fear and uncertainty make it difficult for some to see beyond their immediate circumstances.

Courage isn't something that just happens. Courage is a lot like a muscle. To have strong courage through your leadership challenges, you must develop the attitude, skill and ability to use it.

Here are five attitudes that can help you develop your courage muscle:

1. **Know yourself.** It's difficult to have courage when you're unclear of your guiding values and principles. What do you stand for? Being attuned to who you are is like the foundation of a house. It holds you firm when the demands of leadership challenge you.

2. Do what's right, not what feels good. Often, courage means making uncomfortable choices. A difficult decision won't always feel good in the moment, but if you're connected with your principles then you'll know the right course of action. Always remember to maintain an ethical posture in these moments.

3. Be flexible and open to change. If you find yourself saying, "But, we've always done it this way," then you may really be responding to fear of change. Fear is the opposite of courage. Have the courage to corrupt the norm if it means a better outcome.

4. Accept criticism. Naysayers abound, especially when faced with a leadership challenge. Listen to the critics; they may have a valid perspective on the situation. But always do what's right, both from an ethics and principles standpoint, and then choose.

5. Be willing to admit mistakes. There may have been times when you courageously made what you thought was the best decision, only to find later that you were dead wrong. You're human. Mistakes are part of the territory. Be willing to admit when you're wrong. Those wrong turns are learning opportunities to be savored! Embrace them and choose to do differently next time.

Fear and uncertainty make it difficult for some to see beyond their immediate circumstances. When you walk into the grocery store, do you see more grumbling faces than smiles? On the way to work, do you notice the white-knuckle grip of commuters so wound up in stress that they use their vehicles to exert power, even if it's just to be first at a stoplight? They want to at least be ahead of someone.

Maybe you understand how they feel. You've probably lived through up times and down times yourself. Even so, as a leader, it's your responsibility to lead your organization to success in spite of the difficulties that many employees may be experiencing personally. You can do this efficiently and effectively without losing appreciation for individual circumstances. It's simply a byproduct of your attitude.

Instead of seeing the lack in a situation, seek out the opportunities. Rather than dwell on what's wrong, affirm what is right. Recognize that success is about what you can achieve collectively. These are the perspectives that can help you through even the most challenging times.

When you're knee deep in a difficult situation, it's hard to quell your negative desires and thoughts. It may take years of conscious effort and "mind training" to choose differently. Sometimes you will fail. But most times, you will succeed in maintaining an attitude that makes a situation better, not worse.

You can create your own attitude for success. It takes practice and consistent effort, but it's definitely possible and it starts with something very simple: *Change what you feed your mind.*

When you wake up in the morning, what is the first thing you feed your mind? Is it the morning news? Is it the worry of what the day will bring? Most people start their day with dreadful news, whether it comes from the media or internal thoughts. Choose differently.

Tomorrow when you wake up, try this:

- **Think of five things you appreciate** and quietly say, "Thank you for…" Starting with a perspective of gratitude for what you already have (even though it may not be perfect) trains your mind to see the good in your life.

- **Next, think of your #1 goal** and decide on 2-3 actions—big or small—you'll take to move yourself forward on that goal.

- **Finally, spend 20 minutes** reading something inspirational or motivating. Avoid the morning news or tabloid papers. Find a book, blog, or other resource that is positive and instructional.

Success and happiness are choices based on your attitude. A positive attitude frees the mind to be creative and to seek out and realize new opportunities. When life is spinning out of control, your attitude is the one thing you can control. So be courageous, take the reins and go after the results you desire! By doing so, you'll be well on your way to creating a successful turnaround.

No leader has ever been sorry for bringing out the best in people and the organization.

Reactive Change

We now know that change is about personal growth. As a leader you are better equipped to master change in the workplace if you can master change in your personal life. On a different level, these days it seems that the words "business" and "change" go hand in hand. From dealing with regulatory changes and economic shifts to responding to new customer demands and emerging technologies, sudden and externally mandated changes affect organizations of all sizes.

When change is forced upon you, making the shift is often more stressful and more difficult than when you thoughtfully decide to take your organization in a new direction. After all, making a change that you plan for is exciting and filled with opportunity, while making a change due to outside forces putting pressure on you is filled with risk and unpredictability.

Unfortunately, most organizations resist these externally mandated changes and are slow to respond. They fear the risk involved, and as a result they miss many opportunities. Change under external circumstances is scary because your buy-in to the new ideas is often low, and as such, you don't know if the changes you're making are going to work. Additionally, the change may mean you have to alter your company's values or culture, and those sorts of changes don't come easy.

The fact is that embracing any type of externally motivated change requires both courage and planning. Following are some suggestions for making the organizational change process easier and more successful.

- **Assess your company's current talent potential.**
  When dealing with externally motivated change, a good leader needs the emotional maturity to maximize and leverage the strengths of the people within the organization. Depending on the size of the company or department, you may not have daily contact with those you lead. Therefore, take the time

to go back and assess who you have working for you and what skill sets they have. Chances are some will have developed new skills and strengths since they were originally hired. Therefore, determine how the company can best use the people you already have to make the change successful. Most people overlook the talent that's right under their nose and think they need to look outside for the skills to best move the company forward.

Additionally, just because someone was hired for one position and has extensive training in that area doesn't mean he or she doesn't have hidden talents that are ripe for developing. For example, you may have a financial planner who has a flair for marketing. While you probably wouldn't want to move the person from your financial planning department to your marketing department, you could have that person sit in on marketing meetings and offer suggestions on how to best present the organization's changes to customers in marketing messages. Not only are you helping this person stay engaged in the change process, but you're also getting a fresh perspective you may have otherwise lost.

- **If you do need outside talent, hire people who know more than you do.**
  Many times, those charged with hiring people don't want to hire anyone who is strong, assertive, or more knowledgeable than they are. They think these new hires will make them look bad—or even worse, take

their job. In reality, if you hire people who are strong and know more than you do, you're going to fare better during the change process.

The best way to ensure you make good hiring decisions is to look at the strengths and weaknesses you currently have in your department or company, as well as your own strengths and weaknesses. Make a detailed list of both, and then create a profile of the perfect person who would fill in weaknesses or gaps. For example, perhaps you and everyone you lead is strong when it comes to selling skills, verbal communication skills, and accountability, but as a whole you and your team seem to lack organizational skills, follow-up skills, and written communication skills. If so, make sure the person you hire has, above all else, those key skills you are lacking, regardless of what the actual job position is. After all, technical aspects of any job can be taught. Strengths and weaknesses are inherent.

Realize that when the organization does well, everyone looks good, not just one person. However, if the organization fails, people typically look for one person to blame—usually the leader. The only way your company can sustain its momentum during and after the change is to have strong people on board.

- **Create an environment that encourages continuous learning.**

The knowledge you and your people possess has long-term value for the organization. If you stop learning, you stop having the ability to contribute to the continued development of the organization. Learning is vital, because things change so quickly—technology changes, the industry changes, the marketplace changes, etc. You have to keep up and know what's state-of-the-art to stay relevant to customers. Therefore, encourage your staff to attend seminars, read books, and stay abreast of industry news. Yes, you'll need to pay for any costs associated with this learning, but the costs are minimal when you look at the return on investment you'll receive.

Additionally, implement a system whereby people can get internal feedback and mentoring. This could be a formal process, whereby junior people are paired with a more senior person. Or it could be informal where you arrange monthly roundtable meetings or company-wide lunches that bring the various people and departments together for idea sharing. The more learning opportunities people have, the more valued they'll feel, and the more they'll want to contribute to the change process.

- **Hold people to their commitments.**
No change will ever be complete if people abandon their responsibilities midstream. That's why you need to hold people accountable for what they commit to. To do so, first make sure they have the skills needed to do the job. If they don't, there's no way they'll be successful. Next, get everyone to feel some sense of ownership to the task before them. If possible, let

people volunteer for tasks rather than assign them. If that's not possible, then let them create their own plan to complete the tasks, or at the very least, get their input on how the job needs to be done. The more people feel they have control over the job to be done, the more likely they are to complete it.

Finally, you need to monitor their progress and evaluate how they are contributing (or not contributing) to the change process. Realize that monitoring doesn't mean micromanaging. It simply means keeping the pulse of the entire work flow to ensure all the pieces of the process fit together and are getting done. When you find that someone isn't contributing effectively, it usually means he or she doesn't understand the big picture and how the work plays into the overall goal or change. Therefore, you must be willing to confront this person and deal with the problem in a constructive way that gets the work back on track.

- **In messaging, be clear, consistent, and continuous when communicating the vision and goals.** You have to be clear and consistent about the change, about what's occurring, about what needs to occur, and about the vision and goals for the company. Therefore, spell out where the company is going as well as the plan to get there as specifically as possible. Tie each person's role or task back to the overall goal so they can fully understand and embrace the change. Allow people to ask questions and, if possible, to contribute to the message. Again, people buy into an idea more easily if they feel they took part in shaping it.

When you are not clear, consistent and specific, your message gets garbled and people don't understand it. That's when problems happen and change becomes risky. You think you're communicating one thing but no one understands your real message, so they pull in a different direction. That's why you must make sure everyone is on the same page.

Also, don't just relay the message once. You have to consistently revisit it and make sure everyone is still on the same page. And since everyone learns and processes information differently, it may mean you have to communicate the message in various mediums. This can include verbally talking about the change, writing it out in report form, creating a multimedia video that shows the change, or communicating it in any other way that engages the different learning styles of auditory, visual and kinesthetic.

Approach Change Proactively

Change that's mandated from outside factors is often uncomfortable, but this doesn't mean it's a bad thing. In fact, when approached correctly, this sort of change can open your eyes to new possibilities, new customer bases, new revenue streams, and even new product and service offerings. So tackle these externally influenced changes proactively and you'll have the upper hand. Not only will you fare better than your competitors during the change, but you'll also emerge as the marketplace leader. And that's one change you definitely want to occur. No apology necessary!

In Conflict, Everyone Can Win.

One of the biggest challenges leaders face is managing conflict. That being said, you know that conflict in the workplace is inevitable. Yet most people try their hardest to avoid it by tabling hot topics, tiptoeing around issues, and deflecting challenging questions at all costs. They mistakenly believe that disagreement is unhealthy and will create disruption in the organization.

In reality, conflict is natural and needed. Why? Because when you put the subject on the table and have some healthy discussion (even debate) about it, you can see the issue from all sides. Only then can you begin to devise strategies for dealing with the challenge. Ultimately, conflict brings clarity to issues and helps you and your team define the true challenge. With clarity, you can come together on the best ways to make changes and move forward to help the organization grow. In fact, when you encourage conflict and manage it properly, you can promote the organization's long-term success.

Knowing the best ways to manage workplace conflict can enhance group learning and organizational outcomes. It also enables you to limit the negative effects of conflict that may cause dysfunction. Following are some suggestions to make conflict management easier for all.

- *Let everyone know what conflict is and isn't.*
  Most people avoid conflict in the workplace because they don't know what it really is. Realize that conflict

is not about yelling, screaming, cursing, hitting, or demeaning people. That's bullying and something that should never be tolerated. Conflict in business is never personal. Rather, it's about sharing and discussing ideas that might seem unconventional, that might push people into unfamiliar territory, or that might entail re-imagining what the business is. True conflict challenges the status quo, which is really why people want to avoid it.

- *Promote the idea that conflict is vital to a healthy organization.*
  Superficial harmony stifles creativity and innovation. When people feel afraid to voice a concern or contribute an idea, finding creative solutions to challenges is difficult. On the other hand, when opposing, new, or radical ideas are welcomed and encouraged, people feel comfortable contributing to the group. That's when companies find new ways to do something, new systems to implement, and even new business opportunities.

- *Establish rules for dealing with conflict.*
  If people aren't aware of the ground rules, there's no way they can live or work by them. Therefore, establish your own company's rules for dealing with conflict and make sure everyone knows them. If necessary, post the rules on a conference room wall so they are fully visible, especially during high stakes or conflict filled meetings.

- *Focus on one issue at a time.*

  You'll work through the current conflict more effectively if you focus on it and avoid going off on a tangent. Of course, when addressing any challenge, side issues or concerns may come up. While those side issues should be addressed, resist the temptation to tackle everything at once. Leave room at the end of the current meeting to discuss these new issues, or agree to reconvene at another time to work out the newly raised challenges.

- *Build consensus to avoid win-lose thinking.*

  Ultimately, some of the ideas discussed will be implemented while others will not. So it's natural for some people to feel as though they've "lost." Help everyone understand this is not a win-lose situation. End the meeting by reiterating the points made and why certain ideas presented need to be implemented. If possible, ask for everyone to volunteer for tasks that need to be done. People buy into new ideas more easily if they feel they have a role in the idea's implementation. As long as you're able to have a discussion where everyone has an opportunity to put their ideas forward and all the options are considered, people will feel that they've been heard, and that alone goes a long way to eliminating win-lose thinking.

Embrace Conflict

No organization can or should want to avoid conflict, as it's through conflict that you get the opportunity to define and deal with difficult issues in a productive way. Therefore, it's important that leaders set the example in terms of handling conflict. By creating a sense of teamwork and an atmosphere where people are free to voice their opinions, you'll get dialogue, questions, and healthy debate on pressing issues. And when managed properly, conflict can actually lead to group cohesion, personal growth, and long-term success for any organization.

the checklist

Confidence, the practice of communicating clearly and effectively and the ability to recognize conflict and deal with it are essential skills for all leaders. Understanding that genders, cultures and ages each handle them differently is part of the art of leadership.

chapter 9

Taking Up Power

The most common way people give up their power
is by thinking they don't have any.
—Alice Walker, author

Look in the mirror. What does the mirror tell you?
Your attitude is a reflection of what's in your head—what you think, what you see, and what you convey to others.

Janice's Story

There are few major cities in the United States with female police chiefs. Janice Woodson is the first female police chief for a major Midwestern city—a city known for its historic struggle with corruption and for its budgetary woes.

In that difficult environment, Janice manages to exude confidence, calm and purpose. How does she manage to stay in control despite the endless demands on her time, her courage—even her sanity? She keeps her focus absolute. "My life is very simple," she says. "It's about family. That's how I got to where I am and how I stay here."

She was the first of the children in her family to have a job. She helped to support the family. Janice put off going to college so that she could work. When she was 16, she saw a female police officer getting out of a squad car. Seeing a woman in full uniform made a lasting impression on her. There were so few at that time! The city police force was overwhelmingly male. If you don't see it, you can't dream it.

Janice applied for a police officer position and became a cop almost on a dare. The thinking at the time was, "Why would any woman want to be a police officer? That was a man's job."

To get started, she had to take a written test. It was pretty basic. Then there was a background investigation. There was an agility test. You had to get over a 6-foot wall carrying a 160-pound dummy. That was a bit of a challenge for a small woman like herself at 5'4" and 120 pounds!

The year that she took the test, there was no civil rights act that prohibited discriminatory questions or activities. You had to face an oral exam at the end, from a board of officers. They were not especially thrilled at the idea of admitting women. So they would ask questions like, "How long have you been smoking marijuana?" Loaded questions like that were asked to try to trip up the applicants. It was an intimidating environment.

The program extended for eight weeks, six days a week, twelve hours a day. The lunch break was scheduled for an hour and was before physical training, and so most of the recruits didn't eat. They huddled in the locker room. Janice had never seen a bunch of people so scared, and she was one of them. People were in tears. The program was designed to break you down and build you up. It was very disciplined and rigid.

It was Janice's toughness, clearly, that got her through that difficult training. She formed alliances with other trainees to provide mutual support. Her tenacity helped her to gain the respect of her trainers and superiors. The toughness that she learned at home helped to get her through the training.

And what were those early years on the police force like?

There was a lot of gender discrimination. Officers would call in sick to avoid working with the women. Some women were pinned as cowards. They wouldn't get back up. At 19 she grew up really fast. She had to. Once she tried to arrest a man and he just laughed and said,"I have a granddaughter older than you!"

At just 19 with a gun, she thought she was grown up. The truth is that being given a badge and gun is a tremendous responsibility. If you don't know how to manage that, it can lead to a lot of abuse. You have to use power judiciously.

Janice never thought she would be chief of police. As an African American female, she was an unlikely choice for a major city Police Chief. There was a period when she was laid off as a police officer. She went to law school, after being in the private sector for a few years. She practiced law. The relationships and the work ethic she had developed as a young police officer were invaluable. After a number of years away from the force, she was invited back as one of three deputy chiefs. When the incumbent resigned, she was the one of the three that had the broadest range of experience.

The Mayor called her. She was not overjoyed. It was a big responsibility. There were many challenges, e.g., budgetary, legal. And indeed the whole mindset of the department needed to be recast. There were so many issues that needed attention (fixing). She knew she was taking on an awful lot of work. She would need to bring everyone together, build consensus and influence them all to follow her lead.

As the Chief, there was no one she could go to about the decisions she had to make and the challenges she faced. Mentors were few, but she did have her family. They gave her encouragement. There were days when she knew a gorilla was going to jump on her back. The job was very stressful. You have to be careful not to hold it all inside and just blow up.

It is no secret that for women in jobs like this you have to have a lot of stamina. You have to take every "no" and turn it into a "yes." Janice had to ignore gender discrimination just to get anything done. She knew that in her situation, if she became a victim it would be because she allowed it to happen and Janice was not going to accept that.

Powerful women have the confidence to grab a hold of an opportunity, especially one as powerful as Chief of Police, and are willing to do what is

> No one gives you power.

necessary to influence people to move in a direction to make positive change. In Janice's words:

> Your life is what you make it. Like any other pro-
> fession, policing is enjoyable or gloomy according
> to how you think about it. What you give is what
> you get back out of it.

Women and Power

The rise of women into some of society's most powerful leadership roles around the world ranks among the most significant social transformations of our times. Although still underrepresented, powerful women have emerged in midlevel and senior management positions in almost every discipline imaginable. However, issues of power still evoke as much controversy and misconception as ever before. According to the *Huffington Post*, women, although well prepared, still lag substantially behind men in leadership positions. Women are significantly underrepresented as CEOs, on boards of directors and as senior officers of public companies.

So what, exactly, is *power*?

Women don't automatically assume power, nor can power be bestowed upon you. In other words, no one gives you power. Power is strategic and situational. It depends on a number of variables including the current circumstance, the relationship with others involved and the timing. You have to be ready to take it.

Power is multifaceted. It is about being able to effect change by forging alliances, consensus building, galvanizing people, identifying and effectively utilizing resources. If you have the capacity to influence and exercise control over the opinions and behaviors of others, you are exercising power.

Robbins and Judge in their book *Organizational Behavior* contrast leadership and power. They define leadership as focusing on goal achievement, requires goal compatibility with followers and focusing on influence downward. Power, in their definition, is used as a means for achieving goals, it requires follower dependency and it is used to gain lateral and upward influence.

Five bases of power were identified in the 1960s by John French and Bertram Raven in their study, "The Basis of Power." The first three bases of power are categorized as formal power. They include:

- *Coercive power* has been defined as a manager's use of force to compel an employee to follow an order by the use of threat or punishment if the employee does not comply. Coercion implies the application of force. Rather than to influence behavior through persuasion, coercive power is exerted by means of making a person comply based on fear of consequences. Consequence can be such things as withholding resources or using physical constraint. Both of these can be forms of coercive power. Coercive power is most effective when the threat of violence or other punishment is sufficient in itself to get the target to accede to the demand. Examples of such use can be as simple as taking away your teenager's driving privileges as a result of bad grades at school or writing up or suspending a subordinate for an infraction at work.

> Too often, being powerful and owning power can trip you up.

- *Reward power* is conveyed through rewarding individuals for complying with one's wishes. Typical examples are merit pay or bonuses for good performance or a promotion.

- *Legitimate power* is the formal authority to control and use resources based on a person's position in the formal hierarchy. When a person is recognized for her authority in an organization, she has legitimate power. An example of legitimate power may be the CEO who has ultimate responsibility for the success of the organization. It may also be observed in politics where a person ascends to a position of authority through an election process or by appointment.

The fourth and fifth bases of power are categorized as personal power. They include:

- *Expert power* is that gained through extensive knowledge of a particular subject or an area of expertise. Expert power is usually based on the acknowledgement of your intellect and/or academic accomplishment. People are drawn to this type of leader because they are deemed learned in a particular area. They are considered thought leaders. An example of such an individual is the Fund Development Director whose expertise can be used to lead a capital campaign for a new building project.

- *Referent power* is gained as a result of being trusted and respected by others. Referent power is attained when others trust what you do and have confidence in how you handle situations. An example can be a Corporate Compliance Officer who insures that corporate complaints are handled confidentially and resolved as quickly as possible.

As a manager, to be effective in your job, you may use different types of power to make things happen. Effective managers understand how to use their power to influence others to act according to their wishes and to work toward achieving organizational goals. A manager obtains her power from both the organization (formal power) and from herself (personal power). The key to successful management lies in using a combination of formal power and personal power to influence others. To be successful in leadership you have to use your power in such a way as to influence others to act and to motivate them to get things done.

> In most cases, you may ascend to a position of leadership as a result of a combination of these factors. Whether leadership is gained through legitimate, expert, referent or a combination of these qualities, it involves influencing the actions of others.

Knowing who you are is the most critical element in becoming an effective leader. It requires looking through the lens of critical analysis. It's about being in control of yourself first, before you can expect others to follow your lead. It's about having self-confidence and being passionate about your values and beliefs. A good value system can help you to stay on course when the ship gets tossed in the storm.

The ability to wield power can be very rewarding when you are able to achieve organizational milestones. But too often, being powerful and owning power can trip you up. Power in such cases can be misused and even abused, to the detriment of others. This is often referred to as being on a "power trip." Power tripping is usually viewed from a negative perspective and can cause others to lose respect and appreciation for the person in the power position. Consequently, to be a truly effective leader, it is wise to recognize, develop, and refine those personal characteristics that are the mark of a truly powerful person.

Leaders are found in almost every stratum of life—in companies, politics, and in social organizations such as families, groups of friends, etc. Leaders are powerful people because they have the ability to sway the attitudes, opinions and actions of others. Leaders inspire, influence and achieve results.

Developing the right leadership strategy for the people you lead is crucial to getting the results you desire. Therefore, it is important that you strengthen your skills to better influence, motivate, communicate and coach your people.

Much popular literature on leadership is rife with contrasts between leadership and power. But to be an effective leader you have to exercise power to realize the results you are striving to achieve. Inherent in leadership is the ability to bring others along either through the power of persuasion or position.

Below are my **Seven C's for Gaining and Maintaining Power** and for keeping power in its proper perspective.

- **Character.** John Maxwell, author of *21 Indispensable Qualities of a Leader*, states, "How a leader deals with the circumstances of life tells you many things about his character. Crisis doesn't necessarily make character, but it certainly does reveal it. Adversity is a crossroad that makes a person choose one of two paths: character or compromise." Being willing to sacrifice your success, your fortune, and even your life takes guts. Being unwilling to sacrifice your integrity takes character.

- **Courage.** Martin Luther King Jr. once said, "The ultimate measure of a man is not where he stands in moments of comfort and convenience, but where he stands at times of challenge and controversy." According to Maxwell, "Courage deals with principle, not perception. If you don't have the ability to see when to stand up and the conviction to do it, you'll never be an effective leader." Courageous individuals take calculated risks. They hope for the best possible outcome but are prepared for a loss.

- **Commitment.** Every day of your life you face obstacles and opposition. But commitment is the will and strength to keep forging ahead in spite of how many times you are knocked to your knees. It's the ability to accept setbacks as merely temporary inconveniences that get in the way and try to steer you off course. In the long run, however, unwavering perseverance gets you through.

- **Cautious Attentiveness.** A good leader needs to be accurately informed. Be sure you have all the available facts before deciding anything. Carefully consider all options and their possible results before taking action. Thinking through the potential consequences of your decisions often prevents problems from occurring down the road. Having enough information is only part of the equation. When you have all of the information that is available to you, use your intuition to fill in what's missing.

- **Connectability.** Having the ability to understand, work with, and develop relationships with people is the most important quality a leader can possess. You gain power through relationships. Having the ability to look at each person, understand them, and connect with them is a key component in forming positive interpersonal relationships. Developing relationships with key people will expand your sphere of influence, your access to resources, and your capacity to make things happen.

- **Contribution to the Welfare of Others.** One of the greatest attributes of a good leader is her willingness to serve others. Many times people enjoy being in positions of power because of the perks and benefits they are able to get, not because they want to help people. Service should come from the heart if it is genuine. Having the willingness to help other people and to put their needs and desires before your own is reflected in the attitude and actions of a leader.

- **Creative Perception.** Often referred to as vision, creative perception is essential to good leadership. According to Maxwell, "Vision leads the leader. It paints the target. It sparks and fuels the fire within, and draws the leader forward. It is also the fire lighter for others who follow the leader. Show me a leader without vision, and I'll show you someone who isn't going anywhere. At best, he is traveling in circles."

Because everyone has the capacity to lead, each of you is powerful in your own way. In order to stand out, you have to outthink and outperform the competition. This often calls for some wise and inventive footwork for women to achieve and stay in positions of power.

Managerial Significance

- You can Increase your power by encouraging others to depend on you.

- Expert and referent power are more effective than coercion because:
  - They create greater employee motivation, performance, commitment, and satisfaction.
  - The strengths of these two bases are that they emanate from personal power and are not formally assigned.

- Effective managers accept, understand and are successful at maneuvering through the politics of organizations.

the **checklist**

Power is exciting. As a leader, the use or misuse of it has the ability to build any organization, or take it down.

chapter 10

Communication

*Good communication is as stimulating
as black coffee, and just as hard.*
—Anne Spencer, poet and activist

S ometimes it seems not that *Men Are from Mars,
Women Are from Venus,* but that they are from
entirely different solar systems.

One of the most frustrating and at the same time most
interesting aspects of human existence is the constant effort
of trying to figure out what women (on the part of men) or
men (on the part of women) are all about. Sigmund Freud
threw up his hands in despair over his failure to grasp what
females wanted. Women throughout the ages have pretty much
determined they know what it is men want, but since they
can't understand why it doesn't help very much.

It also doesn't help much that the very basis for coming
to understand much of anything, language, is used differently
by females and males.

Barton J. Goldsmith, PhD, is a Los Angeles-area
psychotherapist and management consultant. He shares:

Men and women also have entirely different conversational styles. Women tend to talk faster when they get excited and may interrupt their partners, who are struggling to find the right words. When this happens, the men may lose track or shut down because they feel cut off and are unable to express what they are feeling.

Author and social philosopher Michael Gurian in his book, *What Could He Be Thinking? How a Man's Mind Really Works,* goes so far as to suggest that there is a major difference in the brain structure of males and females. According to Gurian:

Given the different brain structures of men and women, it will come as no surprise that men inherently distrust feelings, and women inherently trust them.

Certainly this is a generalization, yet your personal experience has probably confirmed it.

Goldsmith writes in a column included on the website *EmotionalFitness.net*:

If you think about the men in your life, you'll probably notice that the majority of them don't tend to think of their own feelings as the final comment on an experience. Men don't tend to think it possible that just "feeling" the experience is actually enough. Feelings are often seen by men as something other people experience. Most men have a hard time communicating anything that remotely resembles an emotion.

Why? Because emotions are scary to men, who think much more than they feel and, much of the time, many men don't know what or how they are feeling. So when a woman wants to talk and a guy realizes he has to think and feel at the same time, just the idea becomes a challenge.

"Differences and similarities between the male and female brain are both increasing and decreasing today, depending on where you focus" according to Gurian. "While many men are learning emotional and family life skills their fathers did not have, studies show that, for the most part, the differences in the male and female brain still remain clear. As most of us have learned intuitively in our relationships with the other sex, the maleness and femaleness of the brain is not as changeable as many people might wish."

If fascination, not frustration, is your approach to attempting to fathom the opposite gender, you will probably find at least some satisfaction; it is a truly fascinating area of psychology.

In a *Harvard Business Review* article, "The Power of Talk: Who Gets Heard and Why," Deborah Tannen reveals:

> What is the most important communication skill? Effective Listening!

Communication isn't as simple as saying what you mean. How you say what you mean is crucial, and differs from one person to the next, because using language is learned social behavior: How we talk and listen are deeply influenced by cultural experience. Although we might think that our ways of saying what we mean are natural, we can run into trouble if we interpret and evaluate others as if they necessarily felt the same way we'd feel if we spoke the way they did.

Men use language to give and receive information and to compete. Their language is more direct and less emotional. Men are typically more proficient in giving orders and fixing what they consider to be a problem, according to Tannen in her book, **You Just Don't Understand: Men and Women in Conversation.**

In fact, men seek to always gain or position themselves to maintain the upper hand. They also try to keep others from dominating them. They are bolder and more direct in their conversational styles. In fact, men's communication styles are often viewed as more aggressive and very competitive. On the other hand, women are usually characterized as more passive. They tend not to be as direct and may be perceived as 'tiptoeing' around the issues rather than taking them head on. Women tend to be concerned more with preserving relationships by being more supportive and conciliatory. Women are seen as more polite and more emotional. Women tend to seek more intimacy in their conversation and may be more talkative in private settings, whereas men are much more comfortable than women speaking in public.

The Workplace

A common occurrence twenty years ago was the perception by women of sexism experienced in the workplace. Of course most people would believe that those days are gone—that today all women are treated equally in the workplace.

Well, unfortunately this type of behavior still exists. Take, for instance, what I learned in an interview with Cindy recently.

Cindy's Story

Cindy, an accountant in a predominantly male accounting firm, was annoyed when a senior partner entered a meeting room full of other male colleagues, looked at her briefly and requested that she get him coffee. He sat down, barely looked her way, and joined in with the conversation. Cindy found his behavior to be rude and dismissive. She immediately thought him to be sexist. She made a point not to address the behavior just then but vowed to meet with him later to discuss the interaction. She later found that he treated all staff this way and had singled her out without any preconceived intent. This was just his way of asserting his authority. As a woman among mostly men in a workplace, this type of occurrence can be very disheartening and easily misinterpreted.

There are other ways in which a woman's contribution can fail to be communicated adequately. In a work environment, female employees may come to feel unappreciated by a male boss who does not offer praise for a job well done. And there is nothing more infuriating than having someone else taking credit for your work. This type of shameless self-promotion can create anger and low morale in the workplace.

Generally speaking, men typically have no trouble tooting their own horns. They proudly share their professional accomplishments almost to the point of bragging. Men are usually less shy about taking credit when they have earned it and may even take more than their fair share. Women are more inclusive. They tend to share credit with others more easily.

Communication Competencies

How can you tell if you are a competent communicator?
Women often precede their comments with, "I'm sorry …," causing them to lose credibility with their audience. Saying "I'm sorry" is a killer for effective communication. It undermines your ability to be perceived as a competent, credible leader. It can cause you to lose credibility and clout among those you are attempting to get your message across to. Being a competent communicator is developing an effective, efficient and productive means of exchanging information so that it is understood by your intended communication target. Competent communication must be tailored to fit your current circumstances and environment.

Listen with All Your Senses

What is the most important communication skill?
Effective Listening!
Competent communication begins with being an effective listener. Effective communication requires listening with all five senses. Depending on the circumstance, you have to listen with more than just your ears. To insure that you are getting the complete message, you may have to call upon your sense of sight, touch, smell, and yes, even taste.

How do your senses affect your ability to communicate effectively?

Seeing   When you see something, thinking, intuitiveness, experiences all come into play.

Touching Sometimes words aren't necessary. A touch on the arm, a stroke, the air from a breath sends a message.

Tasting   Tasting and smelling are linked closely. Has there been a time when you smelled something fabulous and your taste buds could taste it?

Smelling   The Social Issues Research Center, in an article "The Smell Report," addresses this issue of how your sense of smell can have an impact on framing your perceptions of others. Specifically it cites:

> The perception of smell consists not only of the sensation of the odors themselves but of the experiences and emotions associated with these sensations. Smells can evoke strong emotional reactions. In surveys on reactions to odors, responses show that many of our olfactory likes and dislikes are based purely on emotional associations.

> The positive emotional effects of pleasant fragrances also affect our perceptions of other people.

Marketing and advertising get this: likeness (visual/see) and fragrance (smell); written words can create tastes, etc.

Every advertising and marketing arm gets this. There are countless experiments where participants were exposed to pleasant fragrances. What they "saw" was instrumental in how they "rated" the product. They tended to give higher *attractiveness ratings* to people in photographs.

"Unpleasant smells can also affect our perceptions and evaluations. In one study that evaluated artists, the presence of an unpleasant odor led subjects not only to give lower ratings to photographed individuals, but also to judge paintings as less professional."

So, let's say as a healthcare professional, you experience a patient initially as unkempt and having a bad body odor. Your first reaction may be a negative one. You may think that the patient is homeless or has a character flaw. Your treatment of the patient may be less enthusiastic than if the patient were clean, well-dressed and odorless. How you communicate with and treat the patient may be greatly impacted by your association with things you have experienced in your life.

Another research study by Rachel S. Herz, assistant professor of psychology at Brown University, indicates odors can affect people's mood, work performance and behavior in a variety of ways. According to the study, in order for an odor to elicit any sort of response in you, you have to first learn to associate it with some event. This explanation for how odors affect us is based on what is known as associative learning, the process by which one event or item comes to be linked to another because of an individual's past experiences.

> As a leader, you need to find ways to determine if your message was received and understood by those it was designed to reach.

How you perceive, or are perceived, in a conversation may be framed by your association of the other person's look, smell or other criteria not necessarily associated with his or her words.

Hearing   So, the next time you are attempting to communicate with another, make sure you are listening with all of your senses. This is not always easy, especially when you have to always be mindful of the need to disassociate your past experiences from the current situation.

Barriers to Listening

There are many other barriers to listening effectively. Here is a list of some barriers to listening and how you can overcome them.

- **Letting your emotions get in the way.** We all react emotionally to a number of different triggering events in our lives. Certain words, gestures, physical characteristics and other verbal and non-verbal cues from speakers may cause an emotional reaction. For instance, today body modification such as tattooing and body piercing, often accompanied with metal jewelry, is all the rage in some circles. Whether considered a form of self-expression or mutilation, there is no denying that these can be a major distraction in such settings as a job interview. It is hard to listen when you are focusing your attention, even unconsciously, on an individual's physical distinctions.

  As a corporate leader, being mindful of your emotional triggers and managing them effectively can improve your listening experience tremendously. Conversely, if you are the person with the physical distractions, be aware that the receiver of your communication may be blocked by all of your "accessories."

- **Already thinking of what you are going to say while the other person is talking.** There is no way that you can be fully attentive to a speaker when you are focused on your next response. As a result, you may miss out on key information. When it's your turn to talk again, you may have missed much of what the other person was saying. Train your brain to calm itself to receive the entire message before forming a response.

- **Focusing on the message and not the messenger.** I am often struck by how often others tend to formulate an opinion about a speaker before they have heard the message. *You may personally find the speaker attractive or unattractive. You may be prejudiced or biased* by race, gender, age, religion, accent, and/or past experiences. You prejudge the speaker's intellect by thinking that she is not very bright or is under-qualified to speak on the subject. Don't be distracted by personal feelings or others' opinions about a speaker. Actively listen to the message and listen for the merits of the conversation. Focus on what the speaker is saying. After all, you just might learn something that you didn't know.

- **Having a closed mind.** Make sure you have all the information before drawing conclusions. It is easy to be presumptuous; mistakenly believing that you know the reasons behind events or that certain facts imply certain things. Get the facts first so that you may be able to speak clearly and confidently about the facts and not your interpretation of the facts. Try to understand why others think about things differently than you. This may help you to gain a better understanding of the speaker and an appreciation for her point of view. There may be an appropriate time later to lend your opinion.

- **Experiencing information overload.** When a communicator tries to impart too much or irrelevant information, it may be difficult to listen attentively. In cases such as these, try to focus on the relevant information, and the key points in the conversation. If you are the speaker, remember that research shows a person may be able to hold only three to seven things in the conscious mind at once. In John Medina's book, *Brain Rules*, he states that people don't pay attention to boring things. Further, you have only seconds to grab someone's attention and only about ten minutes to keep it. In other words, keep it short and simple.

- **Failure to manage external distractions.** External distractions can take many forms. Trying to listen to more than one conversation, listening to the television or the radio, or hearing the email beep on your computer while meeting with someone, are common types of external distractions. You can control these types of noises by simply turning off the ringer on your phone, logging off of the computer, or turning off the television.

    On the other hand, some noises may be unavoidable such as construction outside your window, or loud talking by other people in a neighboring office.

Environmental conditions such as an uncomfortable room temperature, i.e. too hot or too cold, can also be a distraction. If moving to another location is not an option, you will have to manage as best you can by listening more attentively to block out the noise or dressing in layers to deal comfortably with varying room temperatures.

- **Experiencing physical difficulty.** Feeling unwell, tired, hungry, thirsty or needing to use the toilet can make it very difficult to listen effectively. This is often referred to as physiological noise. This type of distraction can range from simply annoying to unbearably painful and can impact the intensity of your ability to listen. If you should experience a physiological distraction and rescheduling is not an option, you may need to concentrate even more on the task of listening.

Effective Oral Communication—another skill you need to master as a leader. To communicate competently also requires being able to recognize barriers to verbal communications so that you can impart your message in a way that it can be adequately received by the listener. Here are some barriers to effective verbal communication and some strategies to overcome them.

- *Don't assume that your listener is telepathic.* No one can read your mind, nor should you expect people to read "between the lines." Communicate with clarity and specificity. A common problem cited in female versus male communication is the fact that a woman assumes that the man in her life understands what's on her mind. However, if you fail to spell it out, this may be cause for a strained relationship based on an inability to communicate effectively with your partner.

- *Speak as if you are speaking to a 7th grader.* According to the Clear Language Group, the average reading level of American adults is at a 7th to 8th grade level. Similarly, a study by the Central Georgia Technical College states that, "The ability to read and write is the basis for all other education; literacy is necessary for an individual to understand information that is out of context, whether written or verbal." As a leader, be sure to know the average level of knowledge of your employees and adjust your language to match that level of knowledge.

- *Don't come across as superior.* This is true even when you are in a position of authority. Too often an attitude of superiority comes across as condescending. The purpose of the communication should be to solve problems. By focusing on the job or the issue, it becomes easier to determine a resolution and the conversation moves away from personal feelings or personal agendas to solving the problem at hand.

- *Generational diversity presents a unique set of challenges in the workplace.* For the first time in history, there are four distinct generations in today's work force. Members of each generation bring different sets of values, attitudes and behaviors. Frequently, this can lead to conflicts and loss of productivity.

The work style of a Mature (Traditionalist) is structured and orderly with a high regard for honesty, respect and conformity. Matures prefer working with a slower pace. Boomers seek instant gratification and personal fulfillment with timely work habits. Boomers value time. Generation Xers are characterized as less formal, brief in their communication and work style, and prefer to work independently. The youngest of the generations, the Millennials, enjoy working in groups, and have excellent technical abilities. Millennials require clear messages and full details.

As a leader, you are charged with responding to the diverse needs of these generations and uniting them under common goals for your organization. This is no small feat, but it is possible.

Written Communication

- *When writing a report, business letter, or other written business document, think carefully about your audience and avoid a "one size fits all" approach.* Mastering written communication skills is important in the workplace. You need to be able to write well in the majority of jobs. The ability to explain yourself clearly and write in plain English can help you to gain credibility in the workplace. It also

> Before you send an email or text, make sure you determine whether it is actually necessary.

increases your stature and the perceived value of your work. Your message should be clear, concise, grammatically correct and structured appropriately. Check the grammar, punctuation and spelling. Many words sound alike but have entirely different meanings. Make sure to use the right word, e.g., here versus hear. Your goal should be to save the reader time and unnecessary effort so that the message is received as intended. Your writing should answer the following:

- ✓ Who is the audience?
- ✓ What is the purpose of the communication?
- ✓ What do they need to know?
- ✓ How much do they already know about the subject?
- ✓ How important is the subject to them?
- ✓ What is their level of interest in the subject?

- *Emails have become a very important form of communication in the workplace.* Because people's inboxes can quickly become overloaded, it is important that your emails be clear and concise. Make sure that before you send an email or text, you determine whether it is actually necessary. Don't send an email when a face to face interaction or a phone call might be more appropriate and timely. Vary your tone and format to address the audience, i.e. senior management versus clerical staff. Be sure to use an attention grabbing subject line that clearly says what the email is about.

Send emails on a need-to-know basis only. Limit the recipient list to only those who have a professional stake in the conversation. Check your spelling, grammar and tone. Your emails are a reflection of you. They are an important indicator of your professionalism, values, and attention to detail.

Put yourself in the place of your recipients. Ask yourself, "How might others interpret the tone of my message?" Keep your message polite. Read, read again and proofread your message before you click "send." Make sure that your email has a professional signature line.

- *For business writing of any type—emails, letters, memos—always use official company letterhead and/ or the official company logo.* Follow the appropriate company protocols for format. Adjust your attitude/ tone to engage the reader and not offend. Make sure to include a specific subject line. Consider the relevant who, what, when, where, why and how of the message. Bulleted or numbered lists help to guide the reader's attention. State what action is necessary and when.

End your communication in a respectful and friendly manner with a "thank you" and an appropriate formality such as Respectfully, Sincerely, or Warmest Regards. Include information on how to contact you if the reader has questions or a desire for additional information. If there are attachments or enclosures, be sure to indicate that in your correspondence.

Competent, effective communication is a learned skill. It gets better with practice and deliberate attention to detail. In a compelling *Forbes* article, "Communicate to Inspire Action, Leadership Secrets of Hillary Clinton," Rebecca Shambaugh reveals what has made Hillary Clinton a great leader and an effective communicator:

> Over the years, and often in full view of a nation, she has developed an admirable ability to face adversity, get knocked down and bounce back. She has a strong track record for staying positive and optimistic, and operating with a sense of purpose and intention through difficult times. She is resilient.

Shambaugh goes on to talk about how these characteristics can be put to use in the workplace.

> To inspire a more resilient work force and achieve key results in our existing business climate, resilient leaders need exceptional communication skills. In addition to being clear, concise and correct, they need to deliver messages that motivate people to deal with complex and disruptive change, particularly during stressful times. To do this, they need to connect to people, and inspire them to feel engaged around a powerful vision or key goals—in spite of unforeseen obstacles and daunting challenges.

What we do know is that everyone is not born a gifted communicator. Media Coach TJ Walker tells us how Hillary Clinton has not always been the best communicator. He characterizes her as an excellent example of how a person's communication effectiveness can improve at any time. He states that in her public speaking she often came across as monotone, robotic and, with too much projection (causing her to be perceived as yelling). With increased speaking opportunities, she has become a very well respected and effective communicator.

the checklist

You can be an exceptional communicator. It takes practice and a willingness to keep going in spite of the obstacles. The wise leader never assumes that the person he or she is speaking with understands and interprets every word, phrase and nuance as it was intended. The wise leader knows that age, culture, even gender can be a factor in how a message is received and understood. As a leader, you need to find ways to determine if your message was received and understood by those it was designed to reach.

chapter 11

Mentoring: An Investment in Others

Mentoring is a method for managing and
motivating people. Through mentoring, people can grow
and become more effective in their jobs.

Have you ever seen, I mean really seen, lightning?
It takes a little luck, but this phenomenon can be
closely observed.

Lightning is an awesome display of the power in nature.
It comes in several different forms, the most common of which
is forked lightning. Quite often these forks appear like the
bare branches of a gigantic tree, incandescent limbs growing
at a fantastic rate, not from earth to sky but in the opposite
direction. From the original bolt, each fork or branch appears
to pass on its energy to the ones that follow.

To me, this passing on of energy serves as an excellent metaphor for the ways in which leadership, good leadership, can and does work among people. I consider myself to be a leader, much more than I am a follower. As such, I see it as my obligation to pass along to others, through my words and my actions, some of my energy, enthusiasm, wisdom, and experience. In other words, to lead them.

Just as I impart some of myself to those who look to me for guidance, like one fork of lightning accepts energy from another, so, too, as I look back do I see people who did the same for me. It has been my good fortune throughout much of my life to be able, especially when I needed it, to find people willing to be mentors to me, to offer advice and guidance. They have helped "charge" me up when difficult situations threatened to "drain" my energy. I feel a tremendous obligation to the mentors I have had in my academic, my professional, and even my personal life. Part of my way of discharging that obligation is to encourage others to be willing to accept mentors into their lives. Sometimes, even the most certain and headstrong among you must look to others for help and guidance.

> In Greek, a mentor refers to a loyal friend and wise adviser.

The term mentor is from the Greek, and refers to a loyal friend and wise adviser. Throughout history mentors have provided counsel to their protégés. By sharing their practical knowledge and expertise, mentors have proven their value at shaping and preparing select individuals long before formal education and workplace training came into existence. Your first mentors were most likely your parents, although not all people who have

> Mentors are persons who make a commitment to make a difference.

children are up to this job. Sometimes nurturing a child from infancy to adulthood is task enough.

Oftentimes, based upon your interests and your goals, you turn to others as mentors. Some happily follow in the footsteps of their parents, but others seek different paths. While some surgeons come from a long line of medical practitioners and some teachers can look back on generations of educators in their family, a rocket scientist is the son of a coal miner or a ballerina's parents are farmers. At some time, someone or something became the igniting rod to follow a path.

Mentors are persons who a make a commitment to make a difference. They are willing to listen and hear. They have the discipline to balance heart and mind. They are not miracle workers, saviors or therapists. Good mentors are advocates, advisers, and role models. To be a mentor, you do not need hours of special training or a degree in psychology.

Very few people achieve much in life by relying solely upon themselves, and in a way I feel sorry for those who do. They have missed out on something very special. I freely admit that a great deal of the successes I have enjoyed would not have been possible without help from others, without the kind words and sage advice of my various mentors. My accomplishments are all the more gratifying because I can and do share the credit with others.

Good mentors, like forks of energy in the sky, can be the "sparks" that push you on to make your life special for yourself and those around you. They can pass on their gifts to you and you, in turn, can pass them on to others.

Pass it on.

Meet Anne Marie Wilson, a Beautiful Mind

In this complex world, loving families are a critical support system to help children reach their potential. When families aren't supportive, you can only succeed by creating alternative support systems. Dr. Anne Marie Wilson is a consultant who advises executives on how to run their businesses. She credits much of her success to her ability to establish networks of people who keep her grounded, something her family wasn't equipped to do when she was growing up.

In the best possible world, all parents would offer their children a supportive environment that allows them to grow into their best possible selves. Adults would not only guide children in their ways of dealing with the world, but also encourage them to explore their own path through the world. To fill society with successful adults, you must provide children with both the discipline to stay on the path to success, and the freedom to define success on their own terms.

Let me introduce you to a friend who missed out on the second half of that equation. Her parents didn't want her to succeed on any terms but theirs. Let's take a look at what that cost her, but also at how she turned it around, by creating her own family of support. Dr. Anne Marie Wilson is the head of a prominent consulting company that gives confidential advice to business people at the top of organizations worldwide.

Anne has made a career out of the belief that everyone, even powerful leaders, has a basic need to surround themselves with people who will support and nurture their capabilities.

This really is my center, I feel called to do this work.

I remember being at a family gathering when I was about 13 and somehow they had us going around

> saying what we wanted to be when we grew up. I
> said I was going to be a biologist. They laughed; it
> was a big joke.

Anne grew up in a pleasant, middle-class Midwestern suburb. The time was the 1950s, when girls were supposed to grow up to be wives and mothers. Anne's family expected her future life to be all about taking care of others. There was no room for her to have her own ambitions.

> My world was very gender constrained. Boys had
> to make it in the world and would have big lives.
> Girls had tiny little lives.

Anne knew early on that her life was going to be bigger than the one her parents had laid out for her, but she also knew she'd have to fight for it. At home, she had no model for the successful future she envisioned, in which she would go out into the world and make her mark on it, a dream reserved for her brother. Although her parents loved her, they tried to confine her to their dreams for her. They hoped their daughter would become a good homemaker, marry an educated man from a good family, support her husband in his career and raise two or three beautiful children. If her education were important, it was only to make her a better wife and mother.

This sounds like toxic love. Toxic love takes place when people close to you offer an outward show of love and support, but on the inside they really want you to remain down in the dumps with them. They may not even realize that they want you to fail. But they do. Too many of your loved ones, family, friends, the people closest to you, give you this kind of toxic support. They say they love you and yet somehow cause you to feel smaller in the same breath.

That's what happened when 13-year-old Anne told her family she was going to be a biologist. They didn't want to hear her true voice; they wanted her to shrink that voice to fit into the tiny life they'd planned for her. How did Anne overcome the obstacle of her family's toxic love? How did she hold onto her belief in a bigger life, in the face of their laughter?

"One of the saving things of my life was that I discovered music," she says. "My first supporters were Bach and Beethoven. My brother was also very musical, and when he was six he began taking music lessons. I was four and I fought like crazy to have a musical education too, even though everything in our lives was gender divided—we had different toys, different household tasks." Her brother learned piano as part of a complete education, which her parents believed every boy should have. Why didn't she learn to cook or sew instead? She finally wore her parents down and they let her learn piano, too, but only because they could still squeeze it into their picture of the ideal wife and mother.

At four, when Anne first heard classical music, it was her first taste of the human potential for greatness. She knew she needed to fight to hang onto that wider world. "I could just hear it, This piece could not have been written in suburban Michigan. I knew there were bigger things out there."

I know from experience that it's nearly impossible for a child to stand up for her dreams without at least one adult in her corner. I asked Anne if anyone besides Beethoven was on her side.

"Shakespeare and Dickens," she says, at first. But as we continue talking, it becomes clear that she had her living champions, too. "My father had a sister, my Aunt Joanna, who lived a very different life. She couldn't stand my parents' world. She didn't come often—she only really got to know me when I was in college—but she saw when I was very young that I was different."

Although Anne didn't see her often, her Aunt Joanna gave Anne a message she needed to hear: There's another world out there, and you will make it. It was the message of a true supporter, so desperately needed in a world of crippling toxic love.

> In a certain way, she was a beacon. . She was doing such a different thing. In a lot of ways, my father was disparaging of her, but I thought she was amazing.

Anne chose to ignore her father's voice when it talked his sister down. She chose to listen to her champion.

So as a child Anne was not absolutely isolated from the world, sitting alone reading Shakespeare and imagining a better life. She had someone on her side, giving her support and inspiration along the way. Just as all successful people remember someone in their past who has inspired and supported them along the way.

> There is a world out there and I'm going.

Lacking support in her immediate family, Anne also needed to find alternative support in her immediate community. Joanna was only around long enough to provide inspiration. What Anne needed was a mentor. Like me, she had a special teacher who helped her reach up to the next rung on the ladder of success. Her eyes still light up as she remembers discovering this ally years ago. Her teacher looked right past the gender thing.

In seventh grade, there was this math teacher,
Mr. Cameron. He noticed that I had a real acuity
for scientific thinking. He found ways to challenge
me. He gave me things to work on that I would really
love. I'm the kind of math thinker that understands
abstraction, as opposed to engineering. He figured
this out. He was an unbelievable teacher.

Anne desperately wanted to break out of the strict
gender roles of the 50s. She wanted to live a life of the mind.
Her family didn't understand that by laughing at her dream
they were being unsupportive. In fact, they may have thought
it would do her no good to encourage her. To them a woman
living a life of the mind was an absurdity. They didn't know
they were creating hurdles for her. In such an environment,
Mr. Cameron's ability to see Anne's true abilities and to
encourage and nurture them was crucial. She needed to
find that support outside her family, if she were going to
survive in an educational world that devalued women.

Anne was blessed to find support when she so desperately
needed it. But she also showed incredible strength in finding
those outside supporters, and in fighting for herself and for
her own vision of what she would make of her life. She still
spent much of her time away from support systems, often
isolated in her own home. At those times, study became Anne's
salvation. It carried her to a place outside her family's toxic
love and it gave her the life of the mind that she craved.
Eventually it became her ticket out of the suburbs and the
narrow life her family had planned for her.

There is a world out there and I'm going.

She was a high school junior when she decided to break out into a larger life. She took the SAT a year early, at the same time as her older brother with whom she'd always competed. She knew that if she wanted to gain access to the world of her early allies Bach and Beethoven, a world on which intellect and talent could make their mark, she would have to fight.

> I marched into my principal's office and demanded
> that I had to go to college.

Anne must have been an unexpected opponent for this man, who doubtless hoped his female students might go on to college, but only as a prelude to becoming well-read and well-bred wives and mothers. He had never before heard a girl demand her education on her own terms. No one in her school, not even a boy, had ever skipped senior year for college. Faced with such an unusual situation, the principal passed the buck. He said she could go early, but only if her parents agreed.

This led to a difficult confrontation for Anne. After all, these were the people who had laughed at her desire to pursue biology just a few years before. But she was determined not to give up. She spent several weeks arguing her case.

> My parents were exhausted because I was being
> impossible, so they finally gave in. I applied and
> got accepted to lots of colleges and I left.

Many years later, the triumph in her voice still rings clear: she won. Not only had she convinced her parents to let her reach out to find a place in the outside world; the outside world appeared ready to welcome her with open arms. All thanks to her persistence.

But ...

Anne had sprung herself loose from the rigid gender-ruled world of her childhood Michigan suburb only to find herself in the gender-ruled world of academia. And she burst into that world at the beginning of a bitterly contested revolution. It was 1969. The women's movement was just beginning to break into America's universities. Women across the country were demanding admittance to places they had always been denied, and Anne was one of them.

> I grew up fighting, but when I went to college it
> was the same in the bigger world. Here I was, I was
> going to be a biologist—that wasn't happening in
> 1969.

Once again, Anne had to stand up against people who looked at her and saw someone who couldn't possibly succeed, who wasn't a person like them, who wasn't a person they could understand. And, once again, she was blessed to find someone to stand in her corner, someone who had the vision to look past her gender and see her mind.

There's a particular reverence we all have for the names of those people who've helped us when no one else would. I hear it in Anne's voice now:

> John was my mentor and advocate. He was an
> older guy, came from German schools. If you look
> back in history, the idea that a woman could do this
> was looked upon as heresy in Germany and France.
> It was related to the church. It was wired into the
> system and the great professors had grown up
> with this tradition.

At first even he bought into the traditional thinking: women could not become biologists.

But when John saw Anne's "Beautiful Mind," he could not deny it. He was willing to fight for her, not only against his colleagues, but against his own deeply ingrained bias. In 1972 he offered her a spot in a graduate program, despite his own cultural background, and despite the deep resistance in American universities to admitting women into math and science. But Anne would need more than one man's belief in her talent to clear the next hurdle.

She would need money. Up to this point, she had been working to support herself in college, but she had always been able to count on some financial support from her father. Back home in Michigan, college was still considered a traditional step along the way to becoming a wife and mother, but graduate school in biology was a different matter.

> Her father wasn't pleased when he heard this. He refused to shell out more money for a level of education he didn't believe would be of any use to her.

> **Young lady, what could you possibly be thinking? Who will ever marry you if you have a PhD in biology?** He told me to get my butt home ... and I didn't go. I was 100 percent cut off.

Back on campus, except for her champion, John, the academic world was as dead set against her entering its ranks as her father was.

> Professors were appalled that they had to let girls in. Throughout this country no women were ever given graduate support to study science.

Why should they support a woman in graduate school, when she won't be able to compete? Why should a woman take a seat away from a man, when she'll just go and have babies? Those were the kinds of arguments with which she became familiar—echoes of her father's voice.

The fact that her father had plenty of money kept her from getting any kind of needs-based financial aid, even though he had cut her off. The university wasn't interested in her private struggles with her chauvinistic family. But this time Anne's grit and determination to succeed were supported by the grit and determination of women across the country that were fighting just like she was. The women's movement was gaining ground. Anne was in the first class of women to receive financial support from UC San Diego to do graduate work.

> Affirmative action forced them to offer women
> graduate support. If the university had not had
> a stipend, I would not have been able to go.

Anne finished her graduate degree at 24 and was invited to join the applied sciences faculty at a prestigious research university. She was the first female faculty member in the university's history. Even by 2005, women made up only 17 percent of the faculty. But back in 1977, when Anne arrived there wasn't even a women's bathroom in the building where she worked.

> I was fortunate that the women's movement
> was happening. I had a sense of historic purpose.
> When you are young you can be audacious. I was
> going to risk because this had to change. It was a
> fight, it was bigger than me.

At this point in the story, Anne sounds like a warrior. But she admits, "I had plenty of self-doubt." She tells me about her first day of teaching. The university had a tradition in which students would come in before class and erase the chalkboard for professors they admired, but it was a tradition that I knew nothing about!

> I was tiny, with long hair, jeans and sandals. My first class walked in, and there I was erasing the chalkboard.
>
> "What are you trying to do, butter up the prof?" someone asked.
>
> "Well, as a matter of fact, I am the professor," I said, turning to face him.
>
> You could have heard a pin drop. Their little world had changed. Here I was, a petite female that had broken through the all-male department. They gave me hell for just being a woman and young at that.

It's hard when you grow up fighting. Sometimes that anger can fuel you and push you to succeed, but sometimes it can keep you from reaching out for help when you need it most. Anne spent many years isolated from many of the faculty and students. But over time she forced herself to seek supporters wherever she could find them.

That skill proved important when, after six years as an academic, she began to feel confined again. She grew eager to enter the business world.

> Academics was a little too narrow for me. I was contemplating busting out, but I didn't know where to find any support.

Once again she proved that she answered to nobody but herself. She knew what she wanted and she went after it. But she also knew she would need help to make the tough transition from academia to the alien world of business. So she made the transition gradually, and kept her eyes open for supportive people. She started by working on a medical research project. Through that project she met a Swedish man who became a mentor. That relationship didn't develop by chance. He became her mentor because she asked him to teach her!

> I have this amazing network of people who really see me, and who encourage me when I get lost.

Soon she was recruited to a major pharmaceutical lab to help the company expand into a new arena. Again, she knew she needed allies, so she cultivated them: she found a woman colleague who helped her discover more about her own abilities. And she lunched regularly with a male colleague who offered her a crucial outsider's perspective on her work.

I would have gotten killed if I hadn't had grounding perspectives.

As her career took her from pharmaceuticals and beyond, she came to realize the importance of finding not just allies, but allies who could offer those "grounding perspectives." What does that mean? When Anne seeks supporters, she insists on truth-telling at the core of those relationships. She believes strongly in the need for leaders to surround themselves with people who have the freedom, and ability, to offer honest feedback. And she believes it's important to develop colleague relationships outside the traditional framework of coworkers, teams and chains of command.

A lot of relationships are instrumental, and there's nothing wrong with that. But in the inner circle of your network it has to go beyond that to be reciprocal. The nature of the commitment goes beyond that to stand for each other's greatness, truth and capacity. If I can't create that relationship, I leave, because that enables me to tell them what I really think.

Now I'm pioneering this field—but I would have thought it was crazy if someone had told me this is what I was going to do. By now, I have this amazing network of people who really see me, and who encourage me when I get lost. I meet with people regularly and I ask for feedback.

But, like Anne, I found supporters within my family. I can still remember my grandmother, my father's mother, going nose to nose with my father—on my behalf. He was thirty years younger than her and a good foot taller, but she didn't let that stop her. My father had just told me, yet again, "You'll never amount to anything!" when suddenly my grandmother appears. She walks right up to him, sticks a finger in his chest, and says, "You leave that child alone. She's OK." Then, right in front of him, she turns to me and says, "Don't you listen to him. You can do anything!" At that moment, that tiny old woman was larger than life. She was my champion! Little did I know that my grandmother was my mentor and advocate.

I was blessed to have such a strong woman in my life. My grandmother enabled me to see that my father's criticism didn't have to define me. And, she gave me honest feedback.

This honest feedback is important in the working world, too. I remember working at the psychiatric hospital, cleaning bedpans. It was a terrible job, and I felt I was above it, but that didn't mean I did it well. I constantly showed up late, walked around with a chip on my shoulder and talked back to my supervisor. Then she took me aside and told me she was ready to fire me, unless I changed my attitude.

When the scale of our world was smaller it didn't matter so much. But today middle-level managers manage things that are bigger than small countries were 25 years ago. The need for people to be doing this is growing with our speed and connectivity. Many people do this naturally, but they don't do it well. Most people are not so isolated that they don't have a network. They just don't take it seriously enough.

Take your network of supporters seriously. Anne has literally written the book on this topic. How can people build these kinds of relationships mindfully, from the very beginning of their careers? What kinds of people should they look for?

> Diversity of perspective is really important. Look for people who are interesting thinkers, who see the world from different places. And remember not to underestimate how interesting or valuable your perspective might be, even though—or especially because—you're young.

There's something about a certain kind of capacity that does have real grit, and it takes a lot to kill it. When you know that about yourself, you have to follow it.

That kind of belief in yourself is the only thing that can get you safely through a minefield of relationships offering toxic love and toxic support. That certainty is what enabled Anne to face up to her parents, her high school principal, the professors who didn't want to admit a woman to their cloistered world ... and everyone else who ever tried to cut her down while pretending to have her best interests at heart.

Trusting myself the way Anne trusted herself has often been an uphill battle. I come back, time and again, to the image of my grandmother poking her finger in my father's chest and telling him he was wrong about me. I was blessed to have her in my life, but I also have had to make the choice, again and again, to recall her compelling voice on my behalf instead of his. Fortunately, I had that grit that Anne is talking about, and it has always been part of my makeup.

God bless my grandmother and Anne's aunt, my elementary teacher Mrs. Kaufman and Anne's 7th grade math teacher. God bless all those people who had the vision to look at us and see not "just a girl," just a girl with cardboard in her shoes, just a girl with a baby, or just a girl erasing a blackboard. God bless those people who've seen our capacity and nurtured it. God bless them because they taught us that we need not apologize for our ambitions and that we should follow our passions. We wouldn't be here today if we hadn't let their voices shout down our doubts.

Mentoring: Paying It Forward

We live in a microwave society where most expect to get what they want—instantly. We're tricked into believing that fame and success can be achieved overnight, if we'll only work harder, longer and faster. We've adopted an "all or nothing" attitude that says we must either succeed or fail, there is no in between.

But there is an "in between," the period between success and failure that for some, lasts for years.

Long ago, there was a six-year-old boy who, having lost his father, was left to take on the brunt of the household responsibilities while his mother returned to full-time work. He helped raise his younger siblings—cooking and cleaning.

This boy would hold several jobs over the course of his adulthood, from service station operator to insurance salesman. He would experience devastating setbacks, financially and personally, throughout his life. But there was one constant; he loved to cook.

Even more, he loved sharing his cooking with others and eventually that giving attitude turned into a thriving business. That boy was Harland Sanders, the man behind a company that today sells more than a billion "finger lickin' good" chicken dinners around the world each year.

The most striking part of Sanders' story is how long his "in between" lasted. It wasn't until he was well into his 60s that the Kentucky Fried Chicken (KFC) brand began to truly be recognized as a success. Prior to this, Sanders was an ordinary man trying to make a good living. He was a lot like you and me.

Sanders' successful restaurant business is based on the secret recipe of his "11 herbs and spices" fried chicken, but the ingredients to his success are not a secret.

Success Ingredient #1: Passion

Despite holding down a variety of jobs, Sanders was passionate about one thing: cooking. He spent a lifetime perfecting his fried chicken recipe and that passion eventually turned into a thriving business.

Do you have a passion? What is it and how can you express it more fully in your life? If you consider yourself to be passion-less, then I suggest spending time looking back on your life to see what excited you in the past. Your passion may be lying in wait, hoping you'll see it.

Take time to clarify your passion. Only then can you begin to produce the behavior that will turn your vision into reality.

Success Ingredient #2: Positive Perspective

At one point in his career, Sanders worked as a service station operator, a profession that couldn't be any further from his passion for cooking! But he didn't let that stop him from sharing his passion. He began serving his homemade meals to travelers who stopped for gas, which sparked a business idea that eventually led to Kentucky Fried Chicken.

What is your perspective? If circumstances are not exactly as you had hoped, are you tapping into your passion to turn it around, or wallowing in negativity? Although external factors may not be ideal, your internal perspective can be just what you need to make it better. You just have to choose to think differently.

The journey to success is not always easy. There may be roadblocks along the way, but remember that everyone has choices in life. You can choose to use your mind as a powerful tool that can work for or against you. No one else is responsible for how you choose to react to your circumstances. Regardless of the challenges you face, you can live a happy, fulfilled and successful life if you learn to use the resources within you wisely.

You are the person with the most power to affect your life! You are the one who decides how to feel about what you are experiencing. You are the one who gets to choose differently.

Do you choose success?

Success Ingredient #3: Perseverance

It didn't happen overnight. Sanders' success was years in the making. There were no shortcuts. He experienced devastating setbacks including the one that became the catalyst for the KFC franchise. His first restaurant business was forced to close and Sanders was left nearly broke. That's when he decided to sell packets of his secret chicken recipe to other restaurant owners. Even then, he didn't experience immediate success. It took several attempts before he succeeded at this

> A successful person practices and teaches understanding, tolerance, and service to others.

new business venture. But his perseverance won out and led to the KFC brand we know today.

Don't give up. Success could be just around the corner. Keep in mind that "slow and steady wins the race." If you've ever heard how runners train for a marathon, you know that their preparation is grueling and takes time. Baby steps are necessary to build the endurance and fitness needed to run 26.2 miles, but perseverance will make it happen. Crossing the finish line and receiving the medal is the reward for all the hours of hard work and advance preparation.

Success Ingredient #4: Philanthropy

Successful people know that you help yourself when you invest in others. There is nothing more emotionally satisfying than when you give much and expect little in return. Having the willingness to support others and to help them along in their journey is reflected in the attitudes and actions of most successful people. A successful person practices and teaches understanding, tolerance, and service to others.

Sanders gave generously of his time and money. He cared deeply about education. Through organizations that he established, he funded scholarships and gave aid to other deserving organizations.

Reach out to others who may be in need. Such acts of human kindness become self-reinforcing because they answer an innate need in all of us to connect with others in a meaningful way. Such actions give value to and help to clarify your life's purpose.

I have found that a successful mentoring experience can be rewarding both personally and professionally. Through mentoring you can learn new skills, gain a new perspective, and make strides in career advancement. Mentoring is a method for motivating and managing people. Through mentoring, people can grow and become more effective in their jobs.

If you are the mentor, you know how important it is to be willing to ask for help. After all, you have probably experienced the need for guidance and support in your career. If you are the mentee or someone seeking a mentor, you know how important a good mentor can be to your career advancement. You may want to work on building self-confidence, developing professional and winning behaviors, enhancing your knowledge, sharpening critical thinking skills and building your support network.

Self-confidence is one of the most important skills you can develop on your journey to becoming a successful leader. Don't be afraid to ask for help. The most powerful and successful leaders ask for help early and often. If you have someone in mind to serve as your mentor, approach him or her with confidence. Don't say, "I am sorry to bother you, but...." Instead, you might approach the individual like this: "Bill, I thought of you when I ran up against this problem." This type of approach shows that you respect and value the individual's expertise, thereby making it more likely he will want to help you address your issue. It also demonstrates that you are conscientious and want to do a good job.

You could finish the conversation by asking, "May I call on you in the future?" Concluding the encounter in this way leaves the door open for further collaboration with the individual and could lead to a very positive mentoring partnership.

the checklist

Success comes from clarity of passion, recognizing that there are no shortcuts, being willing to do the work, and helping others along the way. These lessons are as much for you as they are for those you coach and/or mentor. Share these success ingredients with the others in your life. But more importantly, teach them that popping these ingredients into a microwave doesn't mean instant, ready-in-seconds success. Show them that the "in between" is just as important as the achievement. You have the ingredients. Now you need only to follow the recipe to success.

chapter 12

Severing the Sorry Syndrome

Your attitude is like a fine wine or
a bitter poison. People know from
the first sip the kind of attitude
you carry.

My aunt Priscilla used to tell me, "Your attitude accounts for 90 percent of what you're able to do in life," and my life is proof of that statement. Everyone has behavior patterns today that were formed at an early age. These behaviors and the thought patterns that inform these behaviors were wired into your subconscious and you are often unaware that it has even happened. Sometimes the information is inaccurate or unpleasant. However, it helps to frame your attitude about the people and experiences in your life.

Throughout your life you will continue to receive negative information, but you can learn to filter out those things that are not conducive to your well-being. However, if left unchecked, they can lead to low self-esteem, stress, anger, resentment and other negative emotions. Your attitude is often shaped by these unchecked negative past experiences. It takes a concerted effort to recognize and understand the advent of a harmful attitude, but purging yourself of this heavy baggage can be very rewarding.

As an example, my childhood wasn't perfect. I grew up with few amenities and not a lot of emotional support. For a time, I succumbed to the circumstances of my life. I dropped out of high school and became an unwed teen mother. While other children were being edified with words of success, encouragement and hope, I was fed words of failure, despair and hopelessness. People told me that I would never amount to anything and I believed them. Consequently, the words of others shaped my thoughts and what I believed I could achieve. I felt that I was doomed to a life of failure. My thoughts defined my attitude and my behaviors.

Your mind is like a window that looks out to the world. If your mind is filled with thoughts of negativity, your view of the world will be altered toward this perspective. Of course, the opposite is also true. When your mind is intently focused on the positive, your attitude will shift toward a more positive outlook. Learning to monitor your emotions and attitude are two of the most important steps you can take toward achieving your full potential. Your attitude impacts your relationships, work performance, and every aspect of your life.

> You are in control of your attitude.

Being aware of the need to constantly monitor your attitude increases your awareness. As your awareness increases, it becomes easier to recognize what you are thinking and how you are feeling about the experience. You can then choose to adjust your thoughts and emotional responses and your behavior as it relates to the experience.

Consider this scenario:

You spent months planning a perfect beach getaway weekend. As you pack, you quietly smile in anticipation of time off from a hectic job. You're tickled because you snagged a great deal by paying for the trip upfront. Do you care if it's nonrefundable? Nope, because you're not changing your plans for anything! You check the weather forecast to see if you need to bring a light jacket for the evening. Oh dear, thunderstorms are predicted for the entire weekend. You're immediately filled with disappointment and dread as you think about your plans being washed away by rain.

You are in control of your attitude.

People are unpredictable. Life is unpredictable. In either case, there are too many variables for you to control. As a result, you will face disappointment and frustration. While you cannot always control people or life's circumstances, you can control your thoughts and your attitude—in any situation. With this control you are free to choose your response. In the midst of what may feel like losing control, you actually have it!

There is immense power in knowing that despite the swirl of changing circumstances, you have control. Claim it! The power of choice enables you to see various possibilities, and you can reveal untapped opportunities. Compare this to the reactionary attitude of someone who feels defeated, angry or upset. That person will react and often chooses a path that closes doors, rather than opens them.

You are in control. You can choose to listen to positive self-talk such as self-encouragement and self-motivation, or you can choose to listen to the gremlins we referred to in chapter six and dwell in self-defeat and self-pity.

Your attitude is like a fine wine or a bitter poison. People know from the first sip the kind of attitude you carry. If you have a negative attitude, chances are it came from past baggage such as self-doubt, self-hatred, and low self-esteem. These internal feelings cloud your outlook. They make you toxic like a bitter poison. As a result, people avoid you for fear of being poisoned themselves. You miss opportunities and you're robbed of chances to reach your full potential.

Dr. Barbara Fredrickson, research psychologist, has shown that positive emotions have two important effects: they broaden your perspective of the world (thus inspiring more creativity, wonder and options), and they build up over time, creating lasting emotional resilience. Her research reveals how positive emotions can tip the scales toward a flourishing life.

Everyone has freedom of choice. It's a universal power and is present in all of you. Similarly, each of you experiences challenging times, hurt feelings, heartache, grief, loss, and physical and emotional pain. Things happen. It is inevitable. The key is how you choose to respond. You can choose to be a victor or a victim.

> The **Sorry Syndrome** surfaces from a lack of self-esteem and a feeling of powerlessness.

The *Sorry Syndrome* surfaces from a lack of self-esteem and a feeling of powerlessness. But you can turn it around. The quality of your life is in direct proportion to the choices that you make and how you act on them. Choose to be the fine wine. Choose a positive attitude. Learn to accept yourself and the decisions you make with confidence. Your attitude is your turnaround.

What does it take to sever the *Sorry Syndrome*? It takes a positive attitude and a healthy self-esteem. Below are several strategies for developing these attributes:

- *Embrace your imperfections; you are not perfect.* Successful people learn about themselves to foster excellence in themselves and their organizations. No one is perfect and to expect perfection is a recipe for failure. Instead, strive for excellence and use mistakes and failures as a way to reassess where you are and plot a course for moving forward.

- *Keep your problems in perspective.* Remember that there is always someone out there who is worse off than you are. In the big scheme of things, your own problems may pale compared to those of others.

- *Be authentic.* Act in accordance with the beliefs you support. Do and say what you believe in. Authenticity cannot be turned on when you get to the office and off when you are on your way home at the end of the day. It doesn't work like a light switch. Authenticity is about being yourself at all times.

- *Take risks.* Accept that you will make mistakes or fail occasionally. It is impossible to live without failing at something. When it happens, it can build confidence and resilience. Success comes most surely and enduringly to those who understand and derive the value from their own failures. Living too cautiously and being afraid to venture outside your comfort zone can cause you to lose out on many opportunities.

- *Develop emotional resilience.* Emotional resilience is important to your health. It is the ability to adapt to crises or stressful situations without lasting emotional damage. Emotional resilience is the ability to "bounce back" after challenging times and life stressors, both major and minor. According to Dr. Andrew Weil, integrative medicine physician, resilient people are able to experience tough emotions like pain, sorrow, frustration, and grief without falling apart. He describes resilience as being like a rubber band. It doesn't matter how far a resilient person is stretched or pulled by negative emotions, he or she has the ability to bounce back to his or her original state. Similarly some resilient people are able to look at challenging times with optimism and hope, knowing that their hardships will lead to personal growth and an expanded outlook on life.

- *Surround yourself with people who get it.* Society encourages you to be strong, independent and self-sufficient. You needn't rely on anyone because you can do it all. This is a trap. Everyone needs support— at the height of success and in the pit of failure.

Everyone needs a network. And it is important to remember that networking is not a numbers game. It's about quality over quantity. Your goal isn't to fill your address book with as many names as possible. Instead, be intentional. Seek out people who are moving in the direction you want to go.

- *Demonstrate unwavering gratitude.* Gratitude means being thankful for the kindness and good will of others and taking nothing for granted. Showing gratitude is good for your physical and emotional health, and your relationships. It is the essence of good mental and emotional health. It can make you happier and more resilient. It can strengthen your relationships, improve your health, and reduce your stress. Dr. Brené Brown, vulnerability expert, has found that there is a relationship between joy and gratitude. She says, "Gratitude is a practice. It must be cultivated and you must keep at it, especially at the lowest points in life." Her twelve years of research has revealed that it's not joy that makes us grateful, but gratitude that makes us joyful.

- *Be a go-giver.* There's a commonly known acronym— WIIFM, or What's in it for me? Sadly, too many people have this attitude about building relationships. Society encourages you to be a "go-getter," but I suggest being a go-giver. If you're not sure what you can give, just ask. Seek to give first and you'll notice your network flourish.

- *Identify and hone your brand.* Do you feel comfortable actively marketing yourself? If not, you are losing too much ground in traveling your road to success. Because who you are matters. You're on the planet for a reason; your work has value. It's time for you to untangle this feeling of shame and self-consciousness from the act of expressing your gifts, and offering your services to the world.

- *Let your light shine!* Women, in particular, have a hard time touting their accomplishments and promoting themselves. We are told, "Don't brag!" "Stop talking about yourself!" But I've learned that it is naïve to think that people will simply take notice of the things you do and your accomplishments. If you want to thrive in your career and you want your work to make a positive impact, you've got to step outside your comfort zone and engage in self-promotion. Selling yourself can feel awkward, arrogant and just plain uncomfortable. Confident self-promotion is the art of spreading your ideas, concepts, and your vision. No one will know what you stand for if you don't tell them. So get comfortable with it and do it!

In the past, my attitude was a bitter poison that negatively affected my life. Until one day, I made a move to change my circumstances. I completed my education and pursued my dream full force. That choice was powerful as I realized how my aunt's statement, "Your attitude accounts for 90 percent of what you're able to do in life," radically changed my life then, and continues to impact it today.

Rather than being sorry for my past mistakes and failures, and letting them rule my life, I chose to embrace them and wear them as my battle scars. They remind me that I have been tried and tested and that I have weathered the storm. I have come out much better for it.

the checklist

My take away for you is this: When you recognize the <u>Sorry Syndrome</u>, you can cure it. Don't apologize for who you are and what you believe in. Instead, be confident in who you are. Stand tall in the knowledge that you are a competent and valuable human being. It isn't always easy. But remember, confidence gives you power. When you fully recognize and appreciate this, you will have taken the first step toward severing the **Sorry Syndrome.**

chapter 13

Final Thoughts

A life consumed with regret can keep you from realizing your full potential. The sheer number of demands and obligations on your time are frequently beyond your control. You can overcome the challenges that this dilemma presents. Know that you will make mistakes, that you are not perfect. No one is! The "Check Lists" presented at the end of each chapter become your resource for building a life of self-confidence, and personal and professional accomplishment. Let me summarize it for you.

Your Check Lists

✓ **STOP ...** Stop apologizing when you aren't wrong. Acknowledge any propensity you have to not offend, make excuses or just using "I'm sorry" as a filler phrase and remove the "I'm sorry" habit. When you do, you will build the skills that you need to become the confident, self-assured woman and leader that you desire to be. Your voice, and you, have the right to take up space in a conversation; claim your positioning within a group and have an opinion.

✓ **Challenges … as a leader, you will encounter them on a daily basis.** With courage, you will be able to accomplish almost anything … and forgive yourself when you make a mistake. It will happen.

✓ **Embrace your purpose.** Simply put, when you discover and follow your purpose, it will change your life for the better and enrich the lives of so many more.

✓ **There are some beautiful, secure, intelligent, and supportive women out there.** Actively seek them out. Don't ever assume that because she is a "she" that she is your closest friend and ally. Close friends and allies are "earned degrees!" Make the choice to continue to move forward and accomplish great things. There are many women who are willing to help you. These women have come to understand that there is enough joy, happiness and success for all to share in.

✓ **Entering the world of work often brings its own degree of uncomfortable attention.** And as a woman, you should be up-front in dealing with it. For starters, you can make it clear to the offender that you are uncomfortable with his behavior. If it persists, you should report it to human resources and/or a superior. If the behavior goes unchecked, filing a formal complaint with the U.S. Equal Employment Opportunity Commission (EEOC) may be your only option.

✓ **Stop, yes, stop and take time for you.** Step back and consider your own needs. You need to learn to stop, take a break, sit down and put your feet up. Apologies for taking time for you are not necessary. After all, the less stress in your life will have a residual effect on everyone else in your life.

✓ **People who master change understand that change happens in life.** They also view change as a learning experience. Change is an opportunity to understand yourself better, redefine your perspective, connect with others and reevaluate your future. Change is about personal growth. When you embrace change and learn from it, you will uncover opportunities to profit from it and use it as a tool to teach others. Change is good.

✓ **Confidence, the practice of communicating clearly and effectively and the ability to recognize conflict and deal with it are essential skills for all leaders.** Understanding that genders, cultures and ages each handle them differently is part of the art of leadership.

✓ **Power is exciting.** As a leader, the use or misuse of it has the ability to build any organization, or take it down.

✓ **You can be an exceptional communicator.** It takes practice and a willingness to keep going in spite of the obstacles. The wise leader never assumes that the person he or she is speaking with understands and interprets every word, phrase and nuance as it was intended. The wise leader knows that age, culture, even gender can be a factor in how a message is received and understood. As a leader, you need to find ways to determine if your message was received and understood by those it was designed to reach.

✓ **Success comes from clarity of passion, recognizing that there are no shortcuts, being willing to do the work, and helping others along the way.** These lessons are as much for you as they are for those you coach and/or mentor. Share these success ingredients with the others in your life. But more importantly, teach them that popping these ingredients into a microwave doesn't mean instant, ready-in-seconds success. Show them that the "in between" is just as important as the achievement. You have the ingredients. Now you need only to follow the recipe to success.

✓ **When you recognize the Sorry Syndrome, you can cure it.** Don't apologize for who you are and what you believe in. Instead, be confident in who you are. Stand tall in the knowledge that you are a competent and valuable human being. It isn't always easy. But remember, confidence gives you power. When you fully recognize and appreciate this, you will have taken the first step toward severing the *Sorry Syndrome*.

You and only you can make the choices necessary to build the life you want. Be courageous. Take charge. There is a life of energy, optimism, and creativity waiting to emerge through you.

Acknowledgments

Writing a book is a major undertaking and can take time. It requires much research, support and assistance to bring together the final product. I was able to pull together a great team of co-creators who saw me through this project; they were people with whom I was able to talk things over, who read, offered comments, or who allowed me to quote their remarks. Several others assisted in the editing, proofreading and the design.

I wish to thank them personally for their inspiration, encouragement and knowledge and other help in creating this book.

I first vetted my idea with Judith Briles, my Book Shepherd. She helped me to clarify and refine my idea and provided suggestions, coaching and editing of my material. This book is much better because of her expertise.

I interviewed a number of succesful women for the various chapters. I am grateful to all of them for taking the time to talk to me about their challenges and successes in the business world. The interviews provided valuable insights that I am able to share with my readers.

Rebecca Finkel of F + P Graphic Design lent her artistry to the cover design and internal layout of the book. She has been delightful to work with through the many revisions.

Debra Benton was my very first executive coach and she taught me a lot about how to *stand in your power* as a leader. These are lessons that I have put to use throughout my career and these lessons will always inform my leadership style. I am so grateful to her for the foreword she has written as well.

A big thanks to all of the wonderful women (and men) who have been my mentors and who have made me see my value as a human being with so much to offer. These include my mother Gladys, my grandmother Daisy, my sister Pam, and last but not least my first grade teacher Mrs. Kaufman. They have taught me much more than can be enumerated here. To each of them I am eternally grateful.

To my husband Chuck, who understands and supports all of my professional pursuits and is always ready with sage advice.

Finally, to my daughters Leantre, Kyla, and LaVeta, and my sister Tamara, you provide the inspiration for my writing.

About the Author

D r. Danita Johnson Hughes is a healthcare industry executive, speaker, author and entrepreneur. Through her professional work, keynotes, writing and philanthropic activities, she inspires people to dream big and understand the role personal responsibility plays in achieving success. As President and Chief Executive Officer, Danita leads Edgewater Systems, an integrated healthcare services system providing behavioral health, primary care and child welfare services to residents of Gary and Northwest Indiana. Her ultimate goal is to help make a measurable difference in community health and well-being. She specializes in organization turnaround and has had much success in giving new life to troubled organizations.

Danita is the recipient of numerous awards including the state of Indiana Governor's Distinguished Hoosier Award. She is a 2013 inductee into the Northwest Indiana Business & Industry Hall of Fame.

Dr. Hughes is a graduate of Indiana University with both a Bachelor's and Master's Degree in Public Administration.

She also holds a Master's Degree in Social Service Administration and a Graduate Certificate in Health Administration and Policy from the University of Chicago. Additionally, she earned a PhD from Walden University.

Active in professional and civic activities, she holds several seats on a variety of boards and advisory councils locally and throughout the country.

She is an avid runner and fitness enthusiast. She has completed six marathons. Dr. Hughes is also an award-winning porcelain doll artist and collector. Her collection consists of more than 300 dolls. She enjoys gardening as well.

Danita is married to Chuck Hughes, and together they have three children, several grandchildren and three dogs.

www.DrDanitaHughes.com

How to Work with Dr. Danita Johnson Hughes

D r. Danita Johnson Hughes speaks and conducts workshops on leadership, women's issues and managing your health for a better life. She is dedicated to helping individuals and organizations function more effectively through better leader-ship and teamwork. Would you like to have her share her wisdom and expertise with your organization or group?

Her topics include:

Women in Leadership

Female executives and CEOs bring a unique perspective to the workplace. Discover the leader within you. Learn what it takes to develop your leadership style and the skills of relationship building and collaboration to accomplish yours and your organization's goals. Learn how women succeed, what holds them back, and how to break through the glass ceiling.

Preparing for Leadership: Do You Have What It Takes to Take the Lead?

Get prepared to take your career to the next level? Learn how to get noticed and selected for a leadership position. Learn techniques for developing effective leadership skills. Discover how to develop a more powerful presence.

The Voice of Leadership: How Leaders Inspire, Influence and Achieve Results

Leadership and effective communication go hand-in-hand with success. Communication is a vital component for creating trust, setting a clear vision and guiding your team to greater performance and profit.

Crossing the Career Chasm: Chances, Choices, and Champions

Awareness of self and others is critical to career success. This topic is designed for people who want to enhance their ability to achieve organizational and career success. Learn to lead through change. Build your credibility, integrity, and influence. Learn the strategies for using personal power to boost your performance.

Practical Principles for Achieving Health, Happiness and Harmony in Life

What are the secrets that will guide you on your own personal journey toward self-fulfillment and wholeness? Make every moment one of great happiness, contentment and peace. Break out of the destructive habits that keep you from having what you really want. Learn the five secrets for achieving health, happiness and harmony.

Defeating the Enemy Within: Ten Steps for Building Self-Esteem

A positive mental attitude and a sense of self-worth are essential to success in every aspect of life. The ten steps will show you how to master the most powerful psychological concepts to develop and maintain a positive mental attitude and healthy self-esteem. Learn affirmations, visualization and behavior modification techniques to help you control your thoughts and achieve your goals.

Power Points for Success

Discover the keys to health, happiness, prosperity and personal success. Increase your ability to be the right person in the right place at the right time to accomplish those things that are most important to your life goals. Change your thinking, change your life, and tap into your own inner resources to achieve confidence, clarity, and control.

Contact Dr. Danita Johnson Hughes

Danita Johnson Hughes would be delighted to participate in your conference or speak to your group. If you want a highly interactive, informative and fun presentation or workshop, call or email her for availability.

Visit her website and explore it: www.DrDanitaHughes.com

Email her at: Danita@DrDanitaHughes.com

Call for Speaker Availability or Consulting: (219) 292-4291

Connect with, share and follow her via social media:

 Danita Johnson Hughes, Ph.D.

 Dr. Danita Johnson Hughes

 @DrDanitaHughes *and*
@TheUnapologeticWoman